KIRKBY STEPH

People, Places and Plague

Upper Eden History Society

Occasional Series: No 1

Best wishes
Charles
from Anne Taylor
July 2019

Published by
Upper Eden History Society
2019

Project Editor: Anne Taylor

Printed in Times New Roman
by Cerberus Printing
Skywalk House, South Road
Kirkby Stephen, Cumbria CA17 4SY

ISBN No. 978-0-9553980-1-8

CONTENTS

ILLUSTRATIONS (where sources are known)

The 'dolphin' logo used by Upper Eden History Society was drawn by Elizabeth Davy. The original small Roman bronze dolphin was found in Westmorland, possibly in Kirkby Thore; it formed part of a group of 120 bronzes bought from a dealer in 1874 by the British Museum. The dolphin is one of a pair, used to secure the shoulder straps of the iron mail shirt of a Roman soldier, and probably dates to the second century AD.

Front cover photographs:
Top left – brockram building stones, Anne Taylor
Top right – Stenkrith bridge, Anne Taylor
Bottom left – Frank's bridge, Ann Sandell
Bottom right – churchyard, Parish Church Kirkby Stephen, Anne Taylor

Back cover, all photographs Anne Taylor:
Top – Plague stone and flowers, near Bluebell Lane Car Park, Penrith
Middle – railings and decorated limestone quoin stones, Kirkby Stephen
Bottom – detail of sandstone quoins, Stenkirth Bridge

Edward Frankland: drawing, Fig. 13, The Workhouse in 1955, page 77. Peter Lewis: photograph, Fig 1, Headstone, Cemetery Kirkby Stephen, page 3. David Mann: photographs, Fig. 1, Plague Stone, just outside Kirkby Stephen, page 125; Fig. 4, The plague stone at Wintonfields, Kirkby Stephen, page 135. Ken Martin: drawings, Fig. 1, How the Workhouse might have looked in the mid-late 19th century, page 45; Fig. 3, First floor landing window; Fig. 4, How the residence might have looked, both on page 52; Fig. 6, The front of the modified workhouse; Fig. 8, Eight-bed female sick ward; Fig. 9, View of the south-facing 'factory' wing – all on page 61. Ann Sandell: drawing, Fig. 2, Town Head Cottages, page 51. Raynor Shaw: Map showing Stenkrith Walking Route, page 36; Map of the Major Fault Ststems in Northern England, page 92; photographs, Fig. 1a to 1d of brockram and buildings, Stenkrith Brockram Walk, page 43; Fig. 3, Roman Road along the Dent Fault System, page 100; Fig. 4, Frank's Bridge in Kirkby Stephen, page 104; Fig. 6, Milkingstile Cottage, Middleton Rd, Brough, page 107; Fig. 7, Smardale Gill Viaduct, page 110. Anne Taylor: photographs, Fig. 2, The plague stone in Bridge Lane, Penrith and Fig. 3, The plague stone near Bluebell Lane car park, Penrith, planted with flowers, both on page 134.

INTRODUCTION
Margaret Gowling

This work is the result of recent research by members of the Upper Eden History Society. Using local sources, found either in the Cumbria Record Offices or among private collections, they have produced some original work illustrating a variety of aspects of the history of Kirkby Stephen and its area. What, for example, happened in the time of the plague? How have the poor been accommodated? What is the connection between transport routes and the local geology? In many cases there is no definite answer and further research is needed. This publication is just a preliminary step in an on-going project in which anyone may join; if you have information you would like to share, please get in touch with Upper Eden History Society via Kirkby Stephen Library at Local Links or the website: http://www.upperedenhistory.org.uk. It is important to preserve information about life in the community, including the small details which do not get a mention in the newspapers yet which give an idea of life in the past, even if the past is only a decade or so ago.

ACKNOWLEDGEMENTS
First and foremost the editor wishes to thank Kathy Lucas who has worked hard on the desktop publishing and David Mann for the Index. Thanks also to all the authors, as well as other members of Upper Eden History Society, and the illustrators and photographers; this has been a long-term team effort. We also thank staff at the Cumbria Archive Centres in Carlisle and Kendal – a publication such as this cannot be produced without their help. However, unless members of the public continue to keep newspaper cuttings, old postcards and other memorabilia there would be fewer archives to consult, so our thanks to all collectors. We are grateful to all those individuals and institutions who have supplied images and given permission for them to be reproduced. We have taken all reasonable steps to obtain permission but apologise for any omissions or errors where owners could not be traced or have been incorrectly identified.

ABBREVIATIONS
CAC (C) – Cumbria Archive Centre, Carlisle
CAC (K) – Cumbria Archive Centre, Kendal
CWAAS – Cumberland and Westmorland Antiquarian and Archaeological Society

PART 1: PEOPLE

Images, clock-wise from top left: illustration by Ken Ormonde, imagining Kirkby Stephen in 1605; advertisement from J W Braithwaite's 1884 Guide to Kirkby Stephen; from the manuscript 'Inventory of the Goods and Chattles of Joseph Shaw of Mallerstang In the Parish of Kirkby Stephen and County of Westmorland' (reproduced with permission of Cumbria Archive Centre, Carlisle).

EGBO – a 19th Century Resident of Kirby Stephen
Peter Lewis

Sometimes there is very little evidence for the local historian. In this article there is a gravestone, and not much more, yet the author has teased out some interesting information about one young individual, buried in Kirkby Stephen.

Some of Egbo's story is speculation; reasonable speculation perhaps, but speculation nonetheless. What is known is that during the mid 1800s Egbo, a young black man from the west coast of Africa, became a resident of the small market town of Kirkby Stephen in the north of old Westmorland. As a young child or adolescent he travelled a long way from home, possibly against his will, to live and work in the town and ultimately die and be buried there.

His detailed personal history is difficult to piece together, there being few tangible clues. One such, however, is the headstone (**Fig. 1**) to his grave in the town's cemetery. Located 35 paces to the south of the cemetery chapel, the inscription reads:

In Memory of
EGBO
of Old Calabar
who died May 20th
1871
Erected by Dr. Henderson

Fig. 1 Headstone Kirkby Stephen Cemetery.

According to the headstone, Egbo's origins were in what was then the Gulf of Guinea coast (now southern Nigeria), in the Efik city-state of Akwa Akpa. This was known to Europeans of the time as Old Calabar, (**Fig. 2**) a name given by 15th-century Portuguese navigators visiting that part of Africa.

It seems that Egbo's tribe, the Igbo, had been the main ethnic group traded out of Old Calabar as slaves, so it is possible he had been part of that trading process, though it was supposed to have been in decline at the time of his birth. Whilst speculative, it is likely that his name Egbo was a misinterpretation or corruption of his tribal name Igbo.

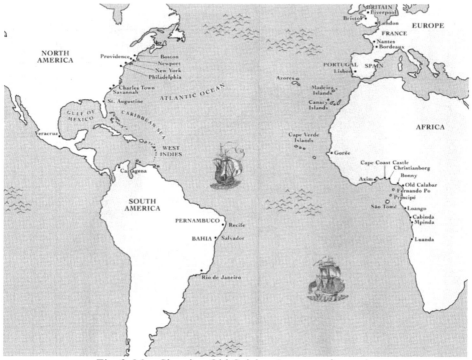

Fig. 2 Map Showing Old Calabar (source unknown)

Most slave ships visiting Old Calabar were English, the majority being from Bristol and Liverpool. The slave trade was banned by a British decree of 1808 and slavery prohibited in all British territories in 1833 following the Abolition of Slavery Act, which took effect in 1834. However, traders from other nations continued to buy slaves from Old Calabar until at least the 1840s.

Where Egbo might have fitted into this network of human trading is difficult to determine, although the 1871 Census described Egbo as:

- a 17 year-old unmarried male;
- an African servant groom from Old Calabon (Calabar);
- residing on Main Street, Kirkby Stephen.

That Census entry places Egbo's birth at around 1854, many years after the supposed cessation of the slave trade; or at least that part of it officially involving British slave traders. Nevertheless it remains possible that Egbo had been caught up in the dying embers of the trade or had, perhaps, travelled with returning colonialists to a new life in their 'mother country', in Westmorland. Local legend has it that a missionary brought him out of Africa (personal communication, Ann Sandell). While this is a rather more romantic notion than Egbo having been a slave, there is no historical evidence to support it and this local belief must join the other possible explanations for his leaving Africa.

Other historical sources (Kirkby Stephen Burial Board Registers, 1861-1976, and Index to Parish Register Transcripts 1861-1984) record that Egbo had been a 'native of Africa' and, as an 18-year-old domestic servant, had been buried in Kirkby Stephen the same day he died. Such a slight variation in age, 17 or 18, does not substantially alter the main narrative.

Whatever the reason for Egbo coming to live on Main Street in Kirkby Stephen, the 1871 Census also records that he shared the residence with the following people:

- Arthur Heslop, boarder, surgeon. Retired. Unmarried, 35 years old, born about 1836. Birth parish Lazonby;
- Thomas H Sayer, medical practitioner. Unmarried. 24 years old. Birth parish Kirkby Stephen. Egbo was described as Sayer's servant groom.

Later sources record that, through to at least 1881, Thomas Sayer was still living on Main Street, had raised a family and continued to work as an MD and surgeon (1881 Census, 1873 Post Office Directory, and 1873 Kelly's Directory). As with the missionary suggestion, it is tempting to think that Egbo accompanied a retiring doctor who had been travelling home to Great Britain. As before, however, there is no historical evidence to support such an idea.

One other piece of Egbo's 'jigsaw puzzle' also comes from his headstone. It records that it was erected by a Dr Henderson. The cemetery's burial book records the purchaser of the headstone/burial plot as a Dr Henderson, executor of the late Mr J Dunkeld (who died in 1867 in Kirkcudbright). Egbo's plot is numbered Row C, 134, burial registration 429. The only traceable Dr Henderson of the period was Joseph Henderson, variously described as a cattle doctor, farrier, blacksmith and, at the age of 71, a veterinary surgeon. As far as can be told there is no further historical record of Dr Henderson. Surmise again of course, but the 'doctor' referred to on Egbo's headstone therefore may well have been a 'cattle' or 'veterinary' as opposed to a 'medical' doctor. There is nothing in the available evidence on which to base any conclusions regarding the relationship between Egbo and Dr Henderson.

The ceremony of Egbo's death and interment was conducted by the Reverend James Simpson LLD, Vicar of Kirkby Stephen Parish Church from 1863 to 1886.

Egbo's death certificate records that, on 21 May 1871 in Kirkby Stephen, Egbo died of smallpox suffocation. Mr Sayer was present at the death when Egbo succumbed to this extremely contagious and deadly virus for which, then as now, there is no known cure. It is possible that Egbo had been a victim of the same smallpox epidemic that had afflicted many of the navvies who had been working on the Settle to Carlisle railway line 1871. Many of the latter were treated in the Kirkby Stephen Workhouse Infirmary, built in the early 1860s, although there is nothing to suggest that Egbo had been cared for there.

So, with a sprinkle of information and a dash of speculation, what is known about young Egbo? He was a young black African male – child, boy or teenager – from Guinea in West Africa who travelled a long way from home either as slave, servant, companion or missionary 'rescuee', to live and work in north Westmorland until his premature death from smallpox at the age of 17 (possibly 18) years on 20 May 1871. Some 147 years or so after his burial and far from home, Kirkby Stephen hosts his body still; he has not been forgotten.

Acknowledgements

With thanks to Helen Bousefield, Chrys Callan, Audrey Dent, Lily Hornby, Valerie Kendall, James Poulson, Ann Sandell and Raynor Shaw.

Sources

Census Records: 1871 and 1881
Cumbria Certificate Services
Electoral Directory 1859
Electoral Directory 1871
Index to Parish Register Transcripts 1861-1984. County Archives, Kendal, reference WDX 1222
Kelly's Directory 1873 and 1894
Kirkby Stephen Burial Board Registers, 1861-1976
Kirkby Stephen Burial Book, 1861-1976
Post Office Directory 1858 and 1873
Sandell, Ann (Personal communication)

TWO FARMERS AND A GENTLEMAN: Hew Shawe, Joseph Shaw and Joshua Tillan
Margaret Gowling

Direct evidence for the lives of ordinary people living in Kirkby Stephen 400 years ago is very sparse, but it is possible to get a glimpse of rural life through these local inventories, drawn up between the late 16th century to the early 18th century. Joseph Shaw's inventory has been selected for the main body of this article because it is legible and detailed, and because Upper Eden History Society holds a copy in its archives. The inventories of Hew Shawe and Joshua Tillan provide a good contrast.

Introduction

The inventory, made soon after the death, was of goods 'moveable and immovable', and therefore excluded land and houses, as well as growing crops. The values were attested by three or four sworn appraisers – local men with the relevant knowledge of the deceased's trade. Inventories were necessary for the probate of a will, and were therefore highly selective; a married woman needed the consent of her husband, and generally only the more prosperous made wills. Probate inventories for Westmorland are lodged with the Cumbria Archive Service, Carlisle, as part of the Diocesan holdings. At present only a few of Kirkby Stephen's inventories have been studied, but a general trend can be observed – over the 150 years under consideration, rural life became less harsh as the economy diversified. The very early inventory of Hew Shawe, which appears in John Breay's book on Mallerstang,[1] is used to set the scene, inventories of Joseph Shaw and Joshua Tillan have been studied at source.

Hew Shawe of Hinging Lunds

Hew, a typical fell-side farmer, died in January 1576/77. His farm, at the far end of Mallerstang, lay on the slopes of Mallerstang Edge, an area of steep slopes and rounded hilltops. It was well above the marshy valley of the Eden. This was one of several isolated farms which had existed from at least the 14th century and subdivided over the years, so that by the late 16th century the land was occupied by many householders with the Shaw surname.[2] Only a very persistent genealogist could unravel the complex family links.

Hew died in January so the inventory necessarily shows his winter stock: a flock of 69 sheep, worth about £10; 8 *kine* [milk cows] and a *stirk* [young beast] worth £9 6s 8d; a few poultry and forty shillings worth of

8

hay. He had also good supplies of food: cheese worth 20 shillings, 2 shillings worth of butter, 8 shillings worth of meal and 10 shillings worth of *fleshe*. In addition he had 9 stones of wool, valued at £3 3s (**Fig. 1**).

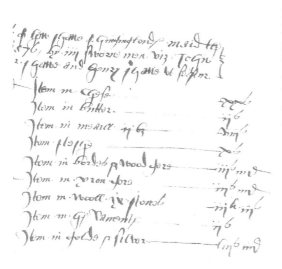

Fig. 1 Part of Hew Shaw's Inventory, reproduced with permission from Cumbria Archive Centre, Carlisle, listing *cheese, butter, meaill, fleshe, in bordes and wood gere, in yron gere, in wool ix stones, in his raments, in gold & silver.*

Living in such an isolated place it was to be expected that this would be at subsistence level. His *raments* [clothing], for example, were *prised* [valued] at just 2 shillings. However, his inventory shows that he had 53 shillings and 3 pence in gold and silver, (**Fig. 1**) and his total assets came to £3 5s. The quantity of wool, long past shearing time, and the value of the cheese suggest at least two saleable commodities. We know that trading in the markets of either Kirkby Stephen or Hawes was possible because the inventory lists a mare. During this period the main route along Mallerstang ran just above his farm (now Lady Anne's Way) to avoid the low-lying marsh.[3]

The items missing from Shawe's inventory are his furniture. Maybe it was all built in, although one would expect forms [benches] and cooking utensils to be mentioned because these were deemed to be the property of the husband, not the wife. They could, however, have been included in the items marked *bordes* [boards], *wood gere* and *yron gere* [wood gear and iron gear].[4] His wife took over the tenancy following his death, but she only survived into the autumn of 1577; her son then took over the lands.[5] John Breay has discussed the development of Mallerstang in detail,[6] so this study now turns to the inventory of Joseph Shaw, who died a century and a half later.[7]

Joseph Shaw, also of Mallerstang
Joseph died in June 1737 (**Fig. 2**). Who was he and what did he do? His occupation is not given, and other sources such as the manor court and parish records are unhelpful, so what can be gleaned from this inventory?

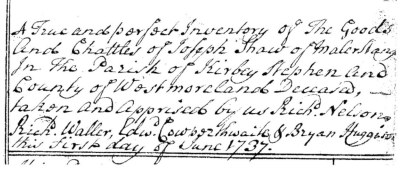

Fig. 2 Part of the inventory of Joseph Shaw, June 1737, reproduced with permission from Cumbria Archive Centre, Carlisle.

Although there is no detail of his estate, he seems to have been comfortably off, well-dressed and with a well-furnished house. His purse and apparel were valued at £13. The amount of ready money he held suggests a trader of some kind. His house was furnished well above his basic needs, with chairs [not just forms], a chest with drawers, [not just chests], a 'seeing glass' and a clock worth 15 shillings. Alongside the brass and pewter ware he had silver spoons and a silver pint. He owned a watch and ten shillings worth of books, so he was probably literate.

Living in Mallerstang he needed to be self-sufficient in foodstuffs. He had two cows and a heffer, plus a *stirk* and three milk cows on his land, as well as seven heffers on the common. These probably produced a surplus, over and above his own household needs. However, he had no sheep. He had husbandry gear and six carts plus two sets of wheels [wheels were luxury items, moved from cart to cart]. There is no mention of hay, which one would expect in June, so his farming may have been curtailed by ill health.

Malt in sacks is mentioned. Had he grown barley,[8] or had he bought in malt for his own brewing? Did he run an inn? But, valued at only £2 3s, this was not sufficient for a working maltster. He not only had a supply of provisions in the house but also fire *elding* [kindling] and peats.

So far the evidence is typical of a small-scale farmer, who had probably disposed of his sheep when he grew too old for the fells. However, he still had a riding mare – a necessity, as shown by the next part of the inventory.

He had scales, weights and *hoseboards*, plus stock[ing?] cards. There was £9 of wool and stockings, and over £14 worth of worsted and yarn hose. These items suggest that he was also a hosier, 'putting out' yarn to knitters and selling the finished stockings to a wholesaler or through the local markets. With his mare, riding saddle, and the carts already mentioned, he could reach the nearby towns. Another clue is the sum of £128 owed to him, which suggests some kind of trading. His total inventory amounted to just over £288. Unfortunately 'debts owing by the deceased as near as can be computed' came to £472 9s 6d.

From this inventory it would appear that he was a small-scale farmer, with a secondary interest as a hosier. Holding so much stock it would appear that he 'died in harness'; he had not retired and one can only hope that another family member could carry on the business.

A different picture is presented by the inventory and will of Dr Joshua Tillan, an inhabitant of Kirkby Stephen town at the beginning of the 18th century.

Joshua Tillan, Gentleman Surgeon
Joshua Tillan/Tillam was an incomer, probably arriving sometime in the 1670s, and died in February 1718. He is not mentioned in the Westmorland hearth taxes of 1670 or 1674, and so far no trace of him has been found in neighbouring counties.

The first mention is with the baptism of his son John, in 1677/78.[9] John was the first of his ten children named in the parish registers of Kirkby Stephen Church, the last was Phoebe in 1699. All the children seem to have survived childhood; the first recorded death was of Sarah, who had been baptised in 1681 and died in 1716. Joshua died in 1718 and his wife Jane in 1723/4.

In addition to his inventory made in 1718, there are other documented sources naming him. He appears as Dr Tillan in local inventories where his services are billed as a surgeon. He also appears several times in the manor court rentals because he acquired land, but his main details come from a court case taken first to Carlisle consistory court and then to York, related to a house he had bought in Kirkby Stephen.[10]

The manor court rentals record that in 1681 Dr Tillan had 'bought off Robert Shaw, a messuage, cowhouse, stable, barn and parcels of land.'[11] The buildings were adjacent to the churchyard wall in Kirkby Stephen. He paid £100 but still had an annual customary rent of 6 shillings, as well as providing a hen and one day's shearing. This was part of a larger property which had belonged to the Shaw family and which they had held since at least 1629.[12] According to evidence given in court, the barn attached to the original house had burnt down thirty or so years earlier and had been rebuilt by Thomas Shaw as a *fire house* [i.e. a dwelling house]. The other part of the property was occupied by the Barnett family, who owned several businesses in the town. When Robert Shaw, the grandson of Thomas, moved down to London, he sold the house to Dr Tillan.

The court case revolved around the ownership of the church pew which went with the property. The case is interesting because it records statements from older inhabitants who remembered the fire, and from the carpenter who had repaired the pew 25 years earlier. The impression is that society had changed little over this period, which covered both the civil wars and the Restoration. Yet this hides subtle changes, for Dr Tillan was not from a local family. As a gentleman, he wished to have the status symbol of being a pew-owner, and as a professional man he was prepared to go through the courts to achieve this aim. Meanwhile, the vendor, Robert Shaw, a member of an old established Kirkby family, had moved, not to Carlisle or York, but to far distant London to make a living.

No judgement has been found for the case, but Dr Tillan continued to buy or rent extra land throughout the rest of his life. He bought the Musgrave lands of Greenriggs, Ingmire and Lady How in 1683.[6] After 1695 he is listed as buying Clifford lands, which lay further afield, such as Angram (Angerholme) at the far end of Mallerstang.[13]

His will shows that at least some of his children married locally and brought up families nearby, as the grandchildren had local surnames.[14] He left his wig to one son and to another his watch, books, gun, sword and the 'plaster box and instruments which were my father's.' Three generations of barber-surgeons! [15]

His inventory reveals an elegant, fashionable existence. His purse, plate and rings were worth over £54, his apparel and purse £14, while his swords, pistols and instruments of surgery came to £6. He also left a cane, a snuffbox and spectacles. He had malt, liquors, brandy and ale to the value of £40.

His house had a clock, pictures, maps and a weather-glass. His professional supplies included medicine, spirits and *oyles*. He also had his own food supply: ham, bacon and beef in the house, plus two *kine* and two swine. He had five horses, and at least two servants were kept because it is recorded that Rowland Simpson and Robert Fawcett were owed £2 16s servants' wages.

His surplus money, over £143, had been lent out in bonds, mainly to local people. One of these, for £45 8s 9d to John Atkinson, may have been part of the purchase price [with interest added?] of Angram, which Atkinson had bought from the doctor. Similarly, Tillan owed Mary Atkinson £80 on bond, again possibly part of a property transaction. He also owed small sums to Mr Pease of Auckland and Mr Baynes of Kendal. Were these perhaps specialised medical suppliers? In all, his inventoried goods came to almost £470 but debts amounted to £255. This is the inventory of a professional man, an incomer, who lived the life of a gentleman, while serving the medical needs of a small rural community in the Upper Eden valley.

These three inventories show what can be ascertained from close study, as well as a knowledge of the historical period and of the surrounding geographical region. Once a simple list of possessions is 'unpacked' it provides a vivid picture of the daily lives of these local men.

NOTES AND SOURCES

[1] John Breay, 1996. *Light in the Dales*. Vols II & III, Norwich: Canterbury Press, Chapter 15. Hew Shawe, 1576, Inventory and Will in CAC (C), D&C wills etc. Also on microfilm JAC 1486.

[2] Breay, 1996. Chapter 14.

[3] 1st Edition Ordnance Survey map, surveyed 1857, printed 1860.WDX 9/0.

[4] *Wood gere* could refer to trestles and boards used at meal times, and the *yron gere* to cooking tools. Information from archivists at CAC (C).

[5] Breay, in Chapter 15, has analysed the changes shown by a selection of inventories of Mallerstang inhabitants during the 17th century.

[6] Ibid.

[7] Joseph Shaw Inventory CAC (C) D&C.

[8] Shaw is unlikely to have grown barley, as hay was the only titheable crop in Mallerstang.

[9] CAC (K) Kirkby Stephen parish registers, WPR 49/1/1. Also WDX 1222/5.

[10] York Borthwick 3665 CP1686-87, at York 1686/7. Carlisle 1685.

[11] CAC (C) D/Mus/1/13/1. CAC (K) WD/HH/1. WD/Hoth/1. Thanet/Clifford Property.

[12] 1629 Thomas Shaw, son of William, rented a house and half a messuage from the Musgrave estate for 7s 5d. a year. CAC (K) Musgrave manor court book WD/Cat/A2095/1 and papers WDX/88/194.

[13] CAC (C) D Mus 1/13/1. WD Hoth/1. Earl of Thanet was owed £2 19s which probably represents rent.

[14] Phoebe kept the medical tradition going by marrying Thomas Grayson of Kirkby Stephen, a physician, in 1722. Kirkby Stephen Parish Registers, Kendal Library (Local Studies).

[15] CAC (C) D&C Will and Inventory 1718. The original wills and inventories are to be found under D&C in Cumbria Archive Centre, Carlisle. Most are also on microfilm.

JOSHUA TILLAN versus HUGH BARNETT
Property disputes in the 17th century: a Kirkby Stephen example
Margaret Gowling

Throughout the country, the 17th century was one of transition from a rural economy to a market-based one. Kirkby Stephen was not exempt from the 'growing pains' experienced by most towns at the time, particularly with regard to the rising demand for residential properties. One particular court case illustrates some of the difficulties that were encountered at this period.

The Court Case: Joshua Tillan vs Hugh Barnett – Carlisle 1685 and York 1686[1]

The Barnett family and the Tillans were neighbours, sharing a property adjacent to the churchyard wall in Kirkby Stephen, originally owned by the Shaws. The actual site is not known: **Fig. 1** shows part of the churchyard and surrounding buildings today. The property had been subdivided following a fire, possibly nearly forty years earlier. The stable that had burned down had been rebuilt as a *fire house* or *mansion house*, which the Shaws had occupied until Robert Shaw sold it to Dr Tillan, 'about nine years ago', [around 1676?] along with three quarters of an acre of arable, adjacent to the house. Stables, which Robert had repaired, were included in the sale. It was stated that 'this was not the original *fire house*'. Tillan had also bought an additional 20 acres from Robert Shaw. In other words, Tillan was trying to establish that he had bought a substantial holding for which he had paid £100.

The original *fire house*, which had not been burnt, had been sold earlier by Thomas Shaw, the father of Robert, to the Barnetts. With the property came one women's pew. Which party was entitled to it?

Fig. 1 The churchyard at Kirkby Stephen Parish Church.

15

The Evidence

Evidence was given by a number of local residents. A few definitions are needed here because their original words have been used where possible: a *fire house* was a dwelling house, and a *mansion house* was a fairly substantial one. A *messuage* is the house and garden.

William Barnett, yeoman, aged 74, stated that he had known the property for sixty years 'and up', and that the seat or pew was originally William Shaw's, as part of his *messuage*. Then Thomas Shaw, his son, had lived in the house and then Robert, his grandson, who sold it to Joshua Tillan.

About 25 years ago, the pew was repaired by himself, William Barnett. He then stated that Thomas Barnett had bought from Thomas Shaw *one cottage house* but he added that this is not the *mansion house*. He repeated that Robert Shaw sold a house and land in Kirkby Stephen and had repaired the stable belonging to the house.

He also pointed out that there had been several seats bought and sold in the church and they should have been recorded in the church book. He added to the confusion by saying that 'the seat was Sewells'.

Thomas Reynoldson, yeoman, aged 75, gave further evidence that the seat had belonged to William Shaw and had then been passed to his son and grandson, and about 20 years ago it needed repairing. He said that in 1640, Thomas Shaw had a stable burned down, which he rebuilt as *a fire house* and now 'it is Joshua Tillan's', and Thomas Barnett bought *a cottage house* off Thomas Shaw.

William Raw, aged 50, had known the pew for 30 years and said that the Shaws had it, and Joshua Tillan bought the property to which it belonged.

Thomas Shaw, aged 50, stated that William Barnett had bought the cottage which was on the site of the barn, about 7 years ago with three quarters of an acre. **John Barnett**, aged 62, and **William Hindmore**, aged 44, both confirmed this.

Geoffrey Thompson, aged 53, also of Kirkby Stephen, agreed that Tillan 'had bought off Shaw,' but stated that Thomas Barnett, who bought the other part of the property adjacent to the church wall, had the section to which the pew belonged. He agreed that Thomas Shaw had pulled the stable down and 'built better' [there is possible confusion between the rebuilding of the barn and the stable]. He continued by saying that Robert Shaw, now in St Martin's-in-the-Fields [London], sold a house to Joshua Tillan along with meadow, pasture, stable and barns.

Comment

The underlying problem seems to have been an expanding population, and consequently a need for more and better houses. The solution, in this case, was the conversion of what had once been one house into two. The confusion had arisen when the burnt-out stable was rebuilt as a substantial mansion while the original house, *the cottage,* was sold off. Later it too was rebuilt. This was not an isolated case; the town was developing southwards – with new buildings like those for the Raw family at Townhead, the subdivision of some *messuages* around the market place, and the infilling of old sites – all examples of the pressure created by the rising demand for residential property.

In 1691 Samuel Shaw,[2] the vicar of Kirkby Stephen, complained of two new houses being built by local men which were encroaching into the churchyard and introducing new problems: the stone caps on their walls directed the water into the thatched roof of his wooden tithe barn. Is this an indication that these new houses were two storeys high and built of stone? The study of the inventories for this period reveals the increasing wealth and specialisation of the householders, yet most of them still maintained their agricultural holdings, particularly if they had commoners' rights, as a safeguard against economic problems. Hence the vicar's worry that if the gates of the new houses were left open, the free-roaming *swines* and cattle would wander into the churchyard and uproot the grass. A further study of local inventories and manor court records might throw further light on this transition from a rural economy to a market-based one, and the development of the town.

SOURCES

[1] Borthwick, York 1686/7. Transmitted causes, 3665 ex CPH1686/3-87. Carlisle 1685.

[2] Churchwardens presentments 29 June 291691. CAC (C) DC. Copy in UEHS archives.

CUMBRIAN ANTIQUARIANS AND THE TAGGY BELL
Anne Taylor

Having heard Kirkby Stephen's parish church clock appear to strike 80 one evening rather than the expected eight, the author turned to 19th century written sources and some present-day Kirkby Stephen residents for information.

Fig. 1 Postcard dated 1926 showing Kirkby Stephen Parish Church, from North Road.

Introduction

Each evening, winter and summer, a bell rings out from Kirkby Stephen Parish Church for many minutes, at around 8pm. Mentioned in almost every book and article written about the town, this is the curfew bell, known locally as the *taggy*. How old a tradition is this? Are curfew bells still rung elsewhere in Britain? Where did the word *taggy* come from? Is it unique to Kirkby Stephen? The answer to the last question is no. It became obvious, with further research, that Penrith had to be included – its curfew bell was also called the *taggy*. The history of both bells is also closely connected with the history of the Cumberland and Westmorland Antiquarian and Archaeological Society.

18

Nineteenth century references to the curfew and the taggy
The earliest reference to a curfew bell rung at Kirkby Stephen seems to be in 1849, in J Walker's *Guide to Kirkby Stephen, being an Imaginary Ramble*. This is a delightful little book describing a stroll through the town – much of which could be done unaltered today. Accompanied by his 'young rambler' Walker imagined climbing to the top of the church tower to admire the view, passing through the belfry in the process.

> *A few more steps, and we shall be at the bells. Now I see them. Come on my friend. That large one there is the death bell, the mournful voice of which has proclaimed the exit of many generations.*
>
> *The one further over is the curfew bell. The term 'curfew' is a compound, or rather an amalgamated corruption of the French verb and noun 'couvre feu', i.e. cover the fire; and you are aware that William the Conqueror, for the security and consolidation of his despotism, made a law that all the people should put out their fires, and go to bed at 8 o'clock in the evening, at which hour a bell was rung to give warning for the covering of the embers, and hence that bell took its original conjunct denomination of 'couvre feu', which was afterwards corrupted to 'curfew'.*
>
> *The 'curfew', which is now the signal for children to go to bed, continues to be rung at Kirkby Stephen to this day.* [1]

The word *taggy* appears a few years later, in 1855, in one of a series of anonymous articles in the *Kendal Mercury* with the title *The People and Dialect of Cumberland and Westmorland*.[2] In fact the author was an Irishman, Jeremiah Sullivan (1820 – 1862), a talented linguist who lived in Penrith and taught in his own private school. He could read Hebrew, Latin and ancient Greek, as well as French, Italian, Spanish, German and the Scandinavian languages. His book *Cumberland & Westmorland, Ancient and Modern: the people, dialect, superstitions and customs* was published in 1857, expanding on the material first presented in his newspaper articles. Part II contains a chapter on vocabulary, with lists of words from Celtic, Anglo-Saxon and Norse. *Taggy* is included in his list of 'Characteristic' Cumbrian dialect words.

> ***TAGGY-BELL*** *(D. täkke, to cover) the curfew or eight o'clock bell, still rung at Penrith and Kirkby Stephen. Cf. couvre-feu, the Norman curfew. Taggy has been used in modern times* [i.e. when Sullivan was writing in the 1850s] *to frighten children; if out after eight o'clock, "Taggy would get them."* [3]

19

This short entry summarises nearly all that is known about the *taggy* bell, even today. Sullivan suggested a possible Danish origin, referred to both Penrith and Kirkby Stephen, and to the personification of *Taggy*. His book was widely praised, and regularly referred to and quoted by other scholars: 'this work places the archaeology of Cumberland and Westmorland in the position merited by the number of antiquities and the importance of the dialect, at the head of the study in England.'[4]

Antiquarians and the taggy
Throughout the second half of the 19th century several other Cumbrian writers commented on the *taggy*. Biographical details are important here because most were members of the newly founded Cumberland and Westmorland Antiquarian and Archaeological Society, CWAAS, founded in 1866 and still thriving today. Three of the founder members – Robert Ferguson, Richard S Ferguson and James Simpson – did much to promote the continued use of local dialect, and therefore the *taggy*.

Robert Ferguson (1817 – 1898) of Morton, Carlisle, was a partner in his father's textile mills at Denton Holme, and MP for Carlisle in 1874. He published *The Northmen in Cumberland and Westmorland* in 1856, very much influenced by the work of a leading Danish archaeologist 'Mr Worsaae' and his 1852 book *An account of the Danes and Norwegians in England, Scotland, and Ireland*.[5] Ferguson's aim was to demonstrate that there were many Scandinavian influences in the north of England; from stones with runic inscriptions to place-names and dialect. In Chapter 10, he included a long list of words of Scandinavian origin: 'my object being to shew [*sic*] that, generally, the Scandinavian element in our language has not been properly represented.'[6] The *taggy-bell* is included, and Sullivan, although unnamed, is given as the only source.[7]

> *TAGGY-BELL. The curfew. So called in the neighbourhood of Penrith, where the custom of ringing the bell is kept up. I am indebted for this word to the writer in the Kendal Mercury, who derives it, and I think correctly, from N. 'tegia', D.' toekke', to cover. Thus the meaning is the same as that of the Norman couvre-feu, or "curfew."*

Richard Saul Ferguson (1837 – 1900) was another Carlisle man. He trained as a lawyer and was the first editor of *Transactions* (the printed record of papers read to CWAAS). He was appointed Chancellor to the Diocese of Carlisle in 1887. In his article on Lanercost Priory in the first issue of the *Transactions*, he wrote: 'So far from William the Conqueror having a footing in Cumberland, the Scots held that county, and, with the exception of a garrison at Carlisle, kept out the Normans until the time of Henry II.'[8]

This strong opposition, particularly in Cumberland, to anything attributable to Norman influence, is evident in the articles of many of the 19th century authors mentioned here. For example, 'where the Norman never set foot'[9] is a quote from Powley 1878, and here is Chancellor Richard Ferguson, in 1882, 1895 and 1897, being praised for 'his laudable efforts' […] 'to keep the name of William the Conqueror out of Cumberland, where when living he never set foot and had no authority. Let not the spirit of William, eight centuries after his death, triumphantly ensconce itself in the tower of Penrith Parish Church.'[10,11]

The Reverend Canon James Simpson (1819 – 1886) was a Westmorland man, Vicar of Kirkby Stephen Parish Church from 1863 until his death, and an important and influential local figure. He was Chairman of CWAAS Council and later its President. His information on the *taggy* bell appeared, not in CWAAS *Transactions*, but in a series of articles written for his monthly Parish Church Magazine. A year or two later, around 1878, Simpson published these articles as a book, *Things Old and New at and around Kirkby Stephen: Westmorland History and Traditions*. No original copies of this publication survive, but it was reproduced in 2006 as part of Upper Eden History Society's 21st birthday celebrations, and is quoted extensively here.[12]

In January 1876 Simpson wrote: *OUR CURFEW BELL. Every night throughout the year, so soon as the Church clock strikes eight, our curfew bell loudly reiterates the fact, and not only so, but goes on deliberately to ring the day of the month. In this respect Kirkby Stephen is not alone. At other places the original purpose has been improved upon in the same way, for example, Carfax, Oxford, where the same custom exists. It is generally supposed that William the Conqueror introduced this custom, but that does not seem to be the fact; He might make some regulations, but the custom itself existed before he invaded England, and has prevailed in other countries as well as our own. The name is said to be from "couvre feu", a kind of reversed coal-skuttle-looking-article used to cover up fires, and thus prevent accidents, in days when houses were constructed of wood. In our own county, before coals were so much used, the fires at night were "raked," that is, "a live peat" was carefully covered with the ashes produced by a hearth fire of turf, or peat, during the day and remained a-light until the morning.*

Simpson wrote again on the theme of bells and local customs in March 1876: *Every Sunday morning immediately after divine service, when the congregation are dispersing, one of our Church Bells (No. 3) is rung for some minutes. This has been the custom "time out of mind" and as the eight o'clock bell is called "The Curfew Bell" so is this called "The Kale Bell" (kele or kyal). This bell was no doubt originally intended to warn those in the town, who had stayed at home to mind the house and prepare the dinner, to set up the kale or broth; those in the more distant villages, to "let down the pot a link." Experience would teach each family how soon, after the ringing of the bell, those of its members who had gone to the Church would arrive at home; and the good wife would so arrange her preparations, that neither her husband's temper not her Sunday dinner should be spoilt by waiting.*

Finally, in September 1876, he wrote about Kirkby Stephen's curfew bell once more: *At eight o'clock on Sunday evening and every other evening in the week, the curfew bell [...] is rung. We may however observe that the local name is "taggy bell," no doubt from the old Danish word "tag," to cover, from which we have thatch, and it was natural enough that the word taggy should be used by Danish people instead of the Norman-French "couvre-feu".*

In the January extract Simpson described two different functions of the bell: to sound the curfew, and to tell the date. However, he gave no indication of how long the curfew bell rang for, nor how to distinguish between curfew and date.

Mary Powley (1811 – 1883) was born at Langwathby in Cumberland, and lived there all her life. Although many of the first members of CWAAS were clergymen and gentlemen, women had been admitted almost from the start and Miss Powley was elected a member in July 1875; she was the first female contributor to the *Transactions*.

In 1877 she read her third paper to the Society, *The curfew bell in Cumberland and Westmorland*, published a year later. She began by saying that 'the sound of the curfew' had not ceased, as was often suggested, and gave a long list of churches as evidence – from Penrith and Kirkby Stephen to Oxford and Shrewsbury. She added that 'in the silence which succeeds its last strokes – usually giving one for each day in the month, which might all of old time be very useful as information – there seems a special solemnity.'[13]

Like most of the other antiquarians, Powley's chief interest was in recording local words and dialect before they died out. She collected several alternative names for the curfew bell and also suggested that the word 'curfew' was less likely to be used in the north. She noted that it was often called the 'eight o'clock bell' and in Newcastle-on-Tyne the 'Thieves' and Rievers' bell' (naming her source as Brockett: *A Glossary of North Country Words* 1846).[14] She acknowledged Sullivan as her source for the *taggy-bell* in Penrith. However, from the way she has recorded this information, it seems that in Penrith the 'threat' of the *Taggy* was already an old tradition, no longer well known in 1877. She wrote '**some years ago**, when old local words became of more interest' Sullivan had heard a 'communication' from the '**late** Mrs Brown' who remembered 'that in her **childhood** [...] **old** persons' threatened children with *Taggy*' [my emphases in bold]. [15]

Reverend Henry Whitehead (1825 – 1896) was born in Kent and was working as an assistant curate in London at the time of the 1854 cholera outbreak. He moved to Cumberland in 1874, becoming Vicar of Brampton, then of Newlands and finally of Lanercost. He was also a member of CWAAS, one of the most 'painstaking and accurate contributors to the pages of its *Transactions*', and wrote extensively on the bells of Cumberland as well as a pamphlet on *The Bells of Penrith Parish Church.*[16] However he acknowledged that his information about the *taggy* came from Powley,[17] and she of course had obtained it from Sullivan. In an article published posthumously, Whitehead mentioned several other evening bells, such as Langham in the East Midlands, and Cockermouth in the Lake District. Although these bells had been discontinued he was interested to find records of small legacies made to fund the evening ringing, and noted that they had only been rung in the winter months.[18]

John Waistell Braithwaite (1849 – 1934) was a Kirkby Stephen man, a 'Printer, Bookseller, Stationer & News Agent' operating from a shop in the Market Place. In the first edition of his *Illustrated Guide and Visitors' Handbook for Kirkby Stephen,* 1884, there are several pages about the church with information on the bells but, significantly, no mention of a curfew bell.[19]

However, later editions of Braithwaite's Guide **do** include a paragraph on the curfew. For example, in a later but undated Guide (probably around 1907) he wrote: 'Kirkby Stephen is one of the few places where the custom of ringing the Curfew Bell has been kept up. [...] After the ringing of the Curfew, the day of the month is rung in numbers on a different bell.'[20]

This seems to be the first reference to the ringing of two bells at Kirkby Stephen, to differentiate between the curfew and the date. Surely this is a first-hand account? Braithwaite's premises were close to the Parish Church and he would have heard the bells every evening. In the *Old Cumbria Gazetteer*, which can be found on-line, there is a reference to Braithwaite's Guide of 1922: 'the eight o'clock bell, the Taggy Bell or Tagg-Bell, was rung on what was the tenor bell of the peal of four, now number 7. It was reported as still being rung in 1922; and after the curfew the number of the day in the month was rung on a different bell.'[21]

Curfew bells today
Simpson mentioned Carfax in his article in January 1876. An internet search has revealed that although Carfax Tower (St Martin's Tower) in Oxford still exists, with a chiming clock and a ring of 6 bells, the bells are only rung occasionally. The curfew bell is not rung today.[22] Powley mentioned 'Great Tom' in Oxford. This is the bell at Christ Church, University of Oxford – still rung 101 times at 9.05 every night.[23]

More pertinent to Kirkby Stephen and the custom of ringing the date as well as the curfew is the following information from Lincoln Cathedral. Just before the cathedral closes, at around 8pm in summer and 6pm in winter, two curfew bells in the north-west tower are rung for a total of 101 strokes. The first bell rings 101 times **minus** the date of the month, and the second bell rings the date. For example, on the 14th of the month the first bell rings 87, the second bell rings 14 (*i.e.* 87 + 14 = 101). There are 101 strokes because of a connection between Oxford University and Lincoln Cathedral.[24]

Another example of a 21st century curfew bell is at the redundant, but still consecrated, St Peter's Church in Sandwich, Kent. Only the tenor bell is safe for ringing, but it is rung by hand every evening – members of the local bell-ringing team taking this duty in turn.[25]

Kirkby Stephen in recent times

The *taggy* continues to be rung in Kirkby Stephen; a hammer strikes the third bell for several minutes every evening at 8 o'clock.[26] Nowadays the mechanism is electronically controlled, but in Canon Simpson's time (as at St Peter's in Sandwich today) it was rung by hand, with a bell-ringer physically going into the church and pulling the bell rope, and in 1870 the bell ringer was Thomas Maugham (**Fig. 2**). Kirkby Stephen's local poet, John Close, recorded: 'And then he *rings our Bells* so fine, The *Taggie-Bell*, so sweet the Chime.'[27]

THOMAS MAUGHAM,
IRONMONGER, WHITESMITH,
LOCKSMITH, AND BELL-HANGER,

Begs respectfully to thank his numerous Customers for their most liberal Patronage, since he opened the above Shop with Goods from the *first* and best Manufacturers, and that he will continue to deal in

Britannia and Metal Tea and Coffee Pots; Copper and other Kettles, and Cutlery of all kinds. (see p. 84).

OPPOSITE SILVER STREET, KIRKBY-STEPHEN,

A Wondrous man of many things,
Bell-hanger—on the best of Springs;
Locksmith—repairs all Locks so fine,
That Maiden Ladies ne'er repine.
His Patent Ovens, none so good—
So strong, so cheap,—be understood.
His *Tombstones* made so very clever,

That once *put in*—will last for ever.
His *Tea-Pots*—Ladies all admire,
Such Tea they brew—none need desire
Better; *Electro-plated* or what not,
More useful Tea-pots can't be got.
And then he *rings our Bells* so fine.
The *Taggie-Bell*, so sweet the Chime.

Fig. 2 Advertisement for Thomas Maugham's shop in Kirkby Stephen, with verses

The bell was rung by hand well within living memory. In the 1950s Miss Lilian Corner (the late Mrs Salter) was the *taggy* ringer. If she was unable to ring the bell, Miss Elizabeth Wright (now Elizabeth Davy) stepped in. Elizabeth does not remember how many chimes were rung, 'perhaps about 30,' nor any instructions to follow the date, but 'it was certainly called the *taggy*'. Elizabeth Davy also recalls that what Canon Simpson called the *Kale Bell* was known to the ringers of the 1950s as the *Pudding Bell*.[28] And several Kirkby Stephen residents remember the bell being rung by Tommy Chamley, who lived in the Workhouse and then at Christian Head.

Several of the older residents remember a time when the *taggy* bell was an important feature in their lives: *children played out all over the town in those days* [i.e. before World War II] *and there were no threats about the taggy man, we just knew that the taggy meant "Leave off playing now and go home" and we did. And a bit later of course, during the War, there were no bells at all.*[29]

Not only is the 8 o'clock bell still referred to as the *taggy*, but the story of the name and the bed-time 'threat' is kept alive in Kirkby Stephen with the opening of a re-named and re-furbished pub – *The Taggy Man*.[30]

The taggy bell in Penrith
There are eight bells in the Parish Church of St Andrew, in the centre of Penrith. Each bell is named – for example number 3 is *Nota*, the 'fire' bell; number 4 is *Signum*, the 'service' bell; number 5 is *Nunaie*, the 'market' bell and number 6 is *Noctula*, the 'curfew' bell.

Early copies of the *Kendal Mercury* and the *Penrith Observer* contain many references to Penrith's *taggy-bell*, most of them quoting Sullivan, Powley, Chancellor Ferguson or Whitehead. All refer to *taggy* as a term used by the 'older generation' and all express a wish to retain this and similar dialect words, e.g. 1897: 'Penrith people [...] would do well to discard the modern innovation of calling their evening bell the "curfew", and restore to it the traditional name of "Taggy".'[31]

A newspaper report of 1916 referred to 'A real curfew at Penrith'. The 'Defence of the Realm Act prohibits the ringing of bells, or chiming from public clocks after dark, and in order to obey that law the Vicar and wardens have arranged to stop the eight o'clock ringing.' However they did not stop ringing the bell, they just changed the timing: 'they will have the bell rung at the exact time required by the Act for the drawing of curtains and blinds, which of course will not be quite the same on any two consecutive days.'[32]

In 1918, the same paper reported on the return of the *taggy* to Penrith – 'I would also like to say how much the older portion of the townsfolk have welcomed the promptness of the return to the eight o'clock curfew or taggy bell as soon as official sanction was given.'[33]

A guide book currently for sale in St Andrew's Church shows a photograph of caretaker, verger and bell-ringer Richard Harriman, who died in 1936. 'Every evening he would climb the tower, and ring the curfew bell.'[34] During the Second World War the ringing of bells was again prohibited and, according to information from the current bell-ringing team, it seems that ringing the *taggy* was not resumed afterwards.[35]

Etymology
Mary Powley was a noted Scandinavian scholar – she was known as *The Cumberland Poetess* and had translated 22 Danish poems into English for her book of poetry *Echoes of Old Cumberland*. In her CWAAS paper of 1878 she questioned other authors' etymological connections between the Danish word *tække* or *täkke* meaning 'to cover' and the Norman *couvre feu* 'curfew'.

She acknowledged the possibility that the word might not come from the Scandinavian or Danish at all, but went on to suggest another Danish word *Taage* meaning mist, gloom or darkness. She quoted a Danish poem on the 'Will o' the Wisp'– *Han lo ad Taage, lo ad Slud, Og cold Natte Vinde* which she translated as 'he laughed at the mist (or darkness), laughed at the sleet, and at the cold night wind.' Powley connected this Danish word *taage* with other northern dialect words such as the Yorkshire 'thaggy' meaning misty or dark, and went on, perhaps a little romantically, to suggest that the 'Taggy' was the 'Bell of the Gloaming, the Mist, or the Darkness' and 'a more natural as well as a more powerful and poetical term, than if it is considered merely as that for the Norman extinguisher.'[36]

In 1892 the *Leicester Chronicle* printed the reminiscences of Mrs Alexander Ireland, born in Penrith: 'the town was so old-fashioned as to ring the curfew or "taggy" bell ("taggy" being evidently cognate with the

German "tag" and English "day") each night at eight o'clock, and still does so.'[37]

All the original sources, including authors such as Sullivan, Powley and Simpson, were writing over 100 years ago. There does not appear to be any recent research on the etymology of *taggy*, probably because the word seems to be restricted today to Kirkby Stephen. Consultation with Richard Dance, a specialist in English etymology, provided the following comment: that *taggy* might 'simply be one of those obscure but expressive local words with no easily identifiable etymology.' Another comment was that the 19th century writers appeared to be looking at 19th century Scandinavian/Danish, rather than the older forms of the language.[38]

Dance also wrote: 'It occurs to me that the word *taggy* perhaps belongs to a set of idiomatic and expressive English formations in 'gg'.' He referred me to another specialist in linguistics, Richard Coates, and his article on the use of the double 'g'. Coates has suggested that words with a double 'g' are a peculiarity of some English words arising from West Germanic forms, particularly words which have their origins in 'pet names' or 'nicknames' and they are not 'attributable to Scandinavian origin or influence.'[39] Would this accord with Mrs Ireland's comment, that the word is related to the German *tag* – perhaps it is just an affectionate name for the 'daily' bell?

In Wright's English Dialect Dictionary of 1905 (see **Fig. 3**) there is a reference to *taggy* as in *taggy-bell*, quoting Sullivan and M.P. (i.e. Mary Powley) as the source of information.[40]

> **TAGGY**, *sb.* Cum. Wm. [ta·gi.] The curfew bell; *gen.* in *comp.* **Taggy-bell.**
> Lakel.¹ So called near Penrith, where the custom of ringing the taggy is still kept up. Cum. Used in modern times to frighten children; if out after eight o'clock, 'Taggy would get them,' SULLIVAN *Cum. and Wm.* (1857) 85; (M.P.); Cum.⁴, Wm. (M.P.)

Fig. 3 The entry for TAGGY in Wright's Dictionary

Wright gave a definition of *tag* as a 'small object hanging loosely from a larger one' or 'the white hair on the point of the tail of a cow or an ox' – in parts of western Scotland a cow with a white-tipped tail was called a *taigie* or *teagie* or *taggie*. Northern English dialect terms are often shared with Lowland Scots[41] and two dictionaries of the Scots Languages (now

28

available on line) covering language in Scotland from 12th century onwards give similar meanings.

Was it the *taggy* because the bell-ringer pulled on a bell rope distinguished by a white *tag*? Was it the 'daily' bell, signifying the end of the day? It seems strange that the word *taggy* was restricted to just two churches, one in Cumberland and one in Westmorland. From 1855 onwards several newspaper articles appeared, mentioning the *taggy*; 15 in the *Penrith Observer* for example. Even if local people in remote Cumbrian villages did not read the papers, their vicars did, and they did not hesitate to respond. However, apart from Mrs Ireland's reminiscences, all quoted Sullivan, Powley, Ferguson or Whitehead.

Perhaps it is a much older northern dialect word, commonly used by the bell-ringers, but has gone unrecorded? Richard Coates is aware that colloquial, 'pet names' such as the *taggy* do not usually 'turn up in ancient documents of the sort historians most often have to deal with' because these documents are often 'legal in character and legalistic in intent.'[42] For example, Whitehead looked at many church accounts in Cumberland, which included payments made to the bell ringers. There were no references to the *taggy,* but often no references to the word *curfew* either. Cockermouth church accounts of 1703-4 record a payment made in November 'for ringing the saven a Clock bell first time 6d.'[43] Any local word used by the bell ringers might not have been recorded in a formal document of more than 100 years earlier. Perhaps it is entirely by chance that the word *taggy* was still in use in Kirkby Stephen and Penrith at a time when antiquarians began to be interested in the dialect of the north, and looking for potential Scandinavian origins.

To conclude on a less academic note – an on-line search of the British Newspaper Archives revealed another author using the word *taggy.* Starting in November 1903 the *London Daily News* published a story by Theodora Wilson Wilson (1865 – 1941), in daily instalments.[44] The main character in the story, Ursula Raven, returned to Westmorland to take up a teaching post, and heard the evening bell. She immediately recognised it: 'she had known the "Taggy bell" since her babyhood – her past was irrevocably bound up with that regular, penetrating beat.' Wilson had been brought up in Kendal and returned there later in life. Had she also read Sullivan, Powley and Ferguson? Or did she know that long ago, one of the Kendal church bells was also called the *taggy*? As so often, when researching local history, one question leads to another.

ACKNOWLEDGEMENTS

My thanks to Ann Sandell and Elizabeth Davy for starting me on this piece of research, to Jo Keogh for up-to-date bell-ringing information, to Audrey Dent for sharing her memories, to Dr Richard Dance at the University of Cambridge for his advice and permission to quote him on the etymology, and to Dr Fiona Edmonds at Lancaster University for comments on Lowland Scots. British Newspaper Archives on-line are now freely available in our public libraries to anyone holding a Cumbrian Library Card – I have made extensive use of this wonderful facility. Thanks also to Cumberland and Westmorland Antiquarian and Archaeological Society – their annual *Transactions* (published in book form since 1874) have been digitized and are freely available via their website: https://cumbriapast.com/cgi-bin/cwaas/cp_main.pl

NOTES AND SOURCES

For most of the background information about the Cumberland and Westmorland Antiquarian and Archaeological Society and its early members I am indebted to *Revealing Cumbria's Past*, edited by M Winstanley, 2016, celebrating 150 years of the Society.

[1] J Walker, 1849. *Guide to Kirkby Stephen, being an Imaginary Ramble*, Kendal: George Lee, p25.

[2] J Sullivan, 27 Jan 1855, *The People and Dialect of Cumberland and Westmorland*, in the Kendal Mercury, p5: 'the curfew of the Normans was translated by the Danes, and in Penrith still retains the name of "taggy bell" (D, *täkke*, to cover).'

[3] J Sullivan, 1857. *Cumberland & Westmorland, Ancient and Modern: the people, dialect, superstitions and customs*, Kendal: Hudson, Dawson & Robinson, p85.

[4] Review of Sullivan's book in the *Kendal Mercury*, 14 Nov 1857, p3.

[5] Robert Ferguson, 1856. *The Northmen in Cumberland and Westmoreland*, London: Longman, and Carlisle: Steel. Introduction p1. See Wikipedia and Wikisource for information about Jens Jacob Asmussen Worsaae.

[6] Robert Ferguson, p163.

[7] Robert Ferguson, p200. Ferguson's book was published in 1856, a year before that of Sullivan, and the newspaper articles were 'signed' *Anonyme*.

[8] Richard S Ferguson and Charles F Ferguson, 1874. Lanercost Priory, *Transactions CWAAS* Old Series, Volume 1, Article XIII, p97.

[9] M Powley, 1878. The Curfew Bell in Cumberland and Westmorland, in *Transactions CWAAS* Old Series, Volume 3, Article XIII, p131.

[10] mentioned by Ferguson to Mr Freeman in a 'visit of the Archaeological Institute to Carlisle in 1882', quoted in Rev H Whitehead, 1895. Church Bells in Leath Ward, No. 4, *Transactions CWAAS* Old Series, Volume 13, Article XXV, p337.

[11] *Penrith Observer*, 30 Nov 1897, Leaves from Northerner's Note Book, p4.

[12] Rev Canon James Simpson LL.D, C. 1878. *Things Old and New at and around Kirkby Stephen: Westmorland History and Traditions.* Reprinted 2006 as *Things New and Old at and around Kirkby Stephen: Westmorland History and Traditions.* Kirkby Stephen: Cerberus Printing Ltd.

[13] Powley, 1878, p128.

[14] Ibid, p132.

[15] Ibid, p130. Sullivan died in 1862, so the story from Mrs Brown must date from over 10 years before Powley was writing.

[16] Obituary of Rev Henry Whitehead, 1897. *Transactions CWAAS*, Old Series, Volume 14, p253. Whitehead played in important part in establishing that cholera was a water-borne disease; an excellent account appears in S Johnson, 2006, *The Ghost Map*, Penguin Books.

[17] Rev H Whitehead, 1895. Church Bells in Leath Ward, No 4, *Transactions CWAAS*, Old Series, Volume 13, Article XXV, pp335-337.

[18] Rev H Whitehead, 1897. Church Bells in Leath Ward, No 5, *Transactions CWAAS*, Old Series, Volume 14, Article XVI, pp309-311.

[19] J W Braithwaite, 1884. *Illustrated Guide and Visitors' Hand-Book for Kirkby Stephen, Appleby, Brough, Warcop, Ravenstonedale, Mallerstang, &Co.*, pp10-11.

[20] J W Braithwaite. *Where to go, What to see,* Kirkby Stephen, post-1906, p8; *A Guide to Kirkby Stephen,* post-1918, p5; and *A Guide to Kirkby Stephen,* dated 1938, p5. Braithwaite became a member of CWAAS in 1908.

[21] This is the only reference I have found to it being called the *Tagg-bell*. I have not found a 1922 copy of Braithwaite; a 1924 edition mentions the curfew and, as with the other editions mentioned above, 'the day of the

month is rung in numbers on a different bell' p5. So far I have found no edition calling the bell the *taggy*. Old Cumbria Gazetteer at http://www.geog.port.ac.uk/webmap/thelakes/html/lgaz/lk18259.htm

[22] From Wikipedia: https://en.wikipedia.org/wiki/Carfax,_Oxford

[23] https://www.chch.ox.ac.uk/visiting-christ-church/tom-quad

[24] Email 20/09/2018 from the Visitor Information Desk, Lincoln Cathedral. Richard Fleming, Bishop of Lincoln, founded the 'College of the Blessed Mary and All the Saints, Lincoln' at Oxford in 1427. See also website: https://thelincolnite.co.uk/2013/11/curious-case-lincolns-curfew-chimes/

[25] Email 01/11/18 from The Churches Conservation Trust, www.visitchurches.org.uk "This bell is indeed still rung by hand. There is a team of ringers, each of whom looks after a 'day' each month." In the past this curfew was called the 'Pigbell' since it 'signalled the time when animals could be put onto the street to eat the rubbish that had accumulated during the day.' The 'Goosebell' used to ring at 5am 'to tell householders to take their animals back indoors lest they be impounded,' but this was deemed to be a too much of a disturbance so early in the day (probably for both ringers and local residents) and has been discontinued. See also: http://www.open-sandwich.co.uk/town_history/traditions.htm.

[26] Jo Keogh, personal communication.

[27] From a verse by Kirkby Stephen's 'Poet Close' (John Close 1816-1891) about Thomas Maugham, seller of teapots and bell-ringer. Printed in The Great Christmas Book 1870-71, 4th advertisement from the back, no page number. Reproduced with permission of Kendal Library.

[28] Elizabeth Davy, personal communication.

[29] Audrey Dent, personal communication.

[30] *Cumberland and Westmorland Herald*, 27 October 2018. 'Taggy Man pub name inspired by folklore.'

[31] *Penrith Observer*, 30 Nov 1897, Leaves from Northerner's Note Book, p4.

[32] *Penrith Observer* 3 Oct 1916, p4.

[33] *Penrith Observer* 19 Nov 1918, p2.

[34] Simon D I Fleming, 1997. *A History and Guide to St Andrew's Church, Penrith*, p12.

[35] Telephone conversations with the President and Secretary of St Andrew's band of bell ringers April 2019.

[36] Powley, 1878, pp130-133.

[37] 'Studies' in *Leicester Chronicle* 9 April 1892, p9. Repeated in 'Penrith Church Bells' *Penrith Observer*, 3 May 1898, p6.

[38] Richard Dance, Director of Studies Anglo-Saxon, Norse & Celtic, University of Cambridge, email to the author December 2018: 'Neither of the two suggestions given here will work as an origin, alas. The 'cover' word is, as Powley notices, cognate with English 'thatch', and in the Viking Age the Scandinavian equivalents would have begun with a 'th' and had 'k' in the middle; cp. OIcel *thekja*. The 'fog' word would have been the same, i.e. as in OIcel *thoka*. (The changes of 'th' > 't' and 'k' > 'g' are both more recent, of course; so comparing modern Danish forms is unhelpful here.)

[39] Richard Coates, 1982. Phonology and the Lexicon: A Case Study of Early English Forms in –gg– *Indogermanische Forschungen* 87, 195-222. In the same article he also wrote: 'you can indeed derive anything from anything else, given a ghost of a mutual resemblance to begin with.'

[40] Joseph Wright, ed. 1905 *The English Dialect Dictionary*, Vol VI T-Z, pp6-8.

[41] Dr Fiona Edmonds, email to the author April 2019, including references to *The Dictionary of the Scots Language* available at http://www.dsl.ac.uk/entry/dost/tag.

[42] Coates, p210.

[43] Whitehead, 1897, p311. One of the church bells was rung every night at seven o'clock for a few minutes, but only during the winter months; so 'the first time' means that the winter ringing started in November.

[44] 'Ursula Raven' by Theodora Wilson Wilson, *London Daily News*, 27 Nov 1903, p13.

PART 2: PLACES

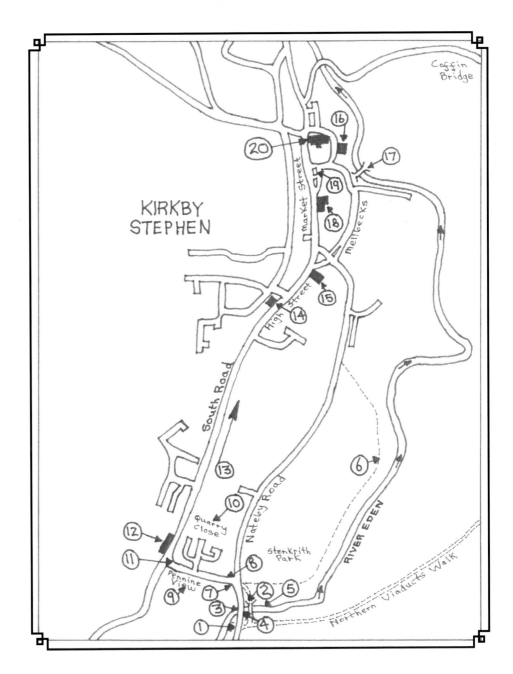

MAP showing the Stenkrith Brockram Walking Route through Kirkby Stephen, drawn by Raynor Shaw, simplified from Ordnance Survey 1:25,000-scale Sheet OL19 Howgill Fells & Upper Eden Valley 2008 Edition.

THE STENKRITH BROCKRAM AND A WALKING TOUR
Raynor Shaw and David Williams

At first glance many of Kirkby Stephen's older houses seem to be built from a rough, reddish-grey stone. A closer look reveals an interesting pinkish hue, particularly noticeable when sunlight shines on rain-washed walls, highlighting the constituent colours. This is brockram, a type of rock that occurs quite widely across Cumbria. The authors set this rock type in its geological context and then describe a Brockram Walking Tour of Kirkby Stephen.

The Origin of Stenkrith Brockram

Brockram is a type of rock known as a breccia[1] in which angular, broken fragments of older rocks have been cemented together. The Stenkrith Brockram, a particular rock-unit that is named after the locality where it occurs, consists of angular fragments of limestone cemented by calcium carbonate, the principal component of limestone (**Fig. 1a**). This distinctive rock-type was formed in desert conditions during the New Red Sandstone Period (about 280 to 200 million years ago). During this Period the limestone rocks, that were originally deposited in shallow tropical seas during the early part of the preceding Carboniferous Period (363 to 325 million years ago), were uplifted to form mountains in a desert environment. Erosion of these mountains created extensive screes and fans of angular limestone debris at the bases of steep mountain cliffs. These fragmentary deposits were eventually buried by later deposits and cemented by lime-rich waters to form the interesting rock that we see today.

Throughout Cumbria, where it crops-out at the surface, brockram has been used to build drystone walls, barns and many of the older houses, either exclusively or in combination with other rock types[2]. Numerous buildings and structures in Kirkby Stephen were built using a brockram that was quarried locally, the Stenkrith Brockram. This short walk, which begins in sight of a natural outcrop of Stenkrith Brockram, proceeds into the centre of the town pointing out various uses of the stone along the way.

The Start

There is a convenient car park (Grid Ref: NY 772 074) on Nateby Road, the B6259, located on the right immediately after crossing the bridge at Stenkrith over the River Eden (**Waypoint 1 on the Map**). Follow the 'Northern Viaducts Walk' footpath that is signposted from this car park. As the footpath levels out under the road bridge, turn left to cross the Millennium Pedestrian Bridge (built 2002) over the River Eden (**Waypoint 2**). The walk begins on this footbridge.

WP	FEATURE
1	Car Park on Nateby Road (B6259) (Grid Ref: NY 772 074)
2	Millennium Pedestrian Bridge over the River Eden (2002)
3	Coup-Kernan Hole in the River Eden
4	Nateby Road bridge abutments (1860-61)
5	Rock platform beside the Eden (optional side-trip)
6	The Poetry Path
7	3.5 metre-high bounding-wall built of Stenkrith Brockram
8	Low wall of Stenkrith Brockram, limestone & sandstone
9	Marshalling yards of the former Stainmore Railway
10	Quarry Close - site of a former Stenkrith Brockram quarry
11	Junction of Station Road and South Road (A685)
12	Former Westmorland Farmers Auction Market building
13	Route down South Road
14	'Old Court House' (1887)
15	Wesleyan Centenary Chapel (1839)
16	The old Grammar School (1566)
17	Frank's Bridge (17th century)
18	Barclays Bank (1903), formerly Martins Bank
19	The War Memorial in Market Square (1920)
20	Kirkby Stephen Parish Church (circa 1230)

Waypoints along the Stenkrith Brockram Walk (as marked on the map)

Exposed Stenkrith Brockram

From the footbridge, look down at Coup-Kernan Hole (**Waypoint 3**) where the river waters swirl around in a complex series of potholes and grooves that have been eroded into exposed Stenkrith Brockram. The geological bed of Stenkrith Brockram is eighteen metres thick at this location, and is inclined (dips) gently southwards. Imagining these layers of rock as overlapping slates on a roof, if one were to follow the River Eden upstream, the rock exposed in the stream bed would give way firstly to the underlying sandstones of the Hilton Series, and next to the underlying (and hence older) Penrith Brockram, a sequence that reveals a fascinating geological history.

Examining Stenkrith Brockram

Fortunately, it is not necessary to climb down to the water level to examine Stenkrith Brockram at close quarters. The abutments (pillars) of the road bridge were built in 1860-61 using Stenkrith Brockram (**Waypoint 4**), with sandstone forming the supporting arch (**Fig. 1b**). Although the left-hand abutment is lichen-covered and the faces of the building stones are obscured, the right-hand abutment is surprisingly lichen-free. Looking closely at the right-hand abutment (**Fig. 1b**) it can be seen that the five-sided blocks that form the arch were skilfully cut from a pinkish-red sandstone. This rock is composed of fine grains of quartz that sparkle in the sunlight as one moves slowly from side to side. In contrast, the rectangular blocks used to construct the abutment are composed of angular fragments of varying sizes enclosed in a finer-grained material (**Fig. 1b**). This distinctive rock is the Stenkrith Brockram. Close inspection reveals that it contains fragments of dull, greyish limestone embedded in a dusty rose-coloured matrix that has been stained by percolating iron-rich solutions (**Fig. 1a**).

Note 1: Although it is not necessary to walk down to the river, during fine weather when the river level is low and the rocks are dry and not slippery, it is possible to walk down to the rock platform beside the Eden (**Waypoint 5**). The first, steeper path to the river begins on the right, beside the Northern Viaducts Trust information board. A second, more gentle path begins a little further on as the main path begins to curve to the left-hand.

Note 2: The Millennium Bridge is also a starting point for the Poetry Path (**Waypoint 6**), which consists of a series of twelve limestone and sandstone boulders with engraved poems that celebrate the attractive scenery of the Eden Valley. The poems highlight the seasonal relationship between traditional fell-farming and the local landscape and wildlife. See https://www.visitcumbria.com/evnp/kirkby-stephen-poetry-path/

THE WALK
Bear in mind that all the walls and buildings along this trail are privately owned, so please respect the privacy of property owners by staying on the public pavement and by avoiding any physical contact with, and damage to, the building stones.

Continuing across the footbridge, the path veers to the left towards two gates in the stone wall that borders Nateby Road. Passing through one of the gates, cross the road to the pedestrian pavement on the right-hand side of Station Road immediately ahead.

To the left is a 3.5 metre high bounding wall (**Waypoint 7**) constructed of Stenkrith Brockram, and to the right is a low drystone wall (adjacent to the 'Pennine View Campsite' signpost). This low wall (**Waypoint 8**) comprises irregularly shaped blocks of Stenkrith Brockram interspersed with random blocks of greyish-white limestone and dull-yellow sandstone (**Fig. 1c**). Notice that although most of the blocks are irregularly shaped 'field-stones', some of the building stones exhibit distinctively saw-cut faces indicating that the wall has been recently rebuilt using leftover building materials.

Heading towards South Road the route passes the Pennine View Campsite on the left (**Waypoint 9**). The Pennine View occupies the site of the former marshalling yards of the Stainmore Railway. This line, which was built to connect the East Coast Mainline at Darlington (via Barnard Castle) with the West Coast Mainline at Tebay, was closed to passenger traffic in December 1952, and finally closed to freight traffic in January 1962.

To the right, opposite the campsite entrance, is Quarry Close. As the name suggests, this housing estate was built on the site of a former Stenkrith Brockram quarry (**Waypoint 10**). This extensive quarry provided most of the building stones for the early houses of Kirkby Stephen.

At the junction with South Road (**Waypoint 11**), the main A685 road, cross over onto the opposite pavement to stand in front of the former

Westmorland Farmers Auction Market building (**Waypoint 12**) that is now occupied by several small local businesses. This building is constructed of Stenkrith Brockram. The long, high walls provide an easily accessible display of the wide variations in composition inherent in this rock-type, formed as it was by the cementing of successive sheets of angular rock-debris. In particular, within and between each building stone notice: a) the contrasting sizes and shapes of the larger contained fragments (the 'clasts), b) the nature of the enclosing 'cement' (the 'matrix'), and c) the interesting colour variations.

From here, the route heads down the hill along South Road (**Waypoint 13**) towards the centre of Kirkby Stephen (**Fig. 1d**). Walking towards the town look at the different materials that were used to build the houses that flank this road. Although many are built from rough, randomly shaped blocks (so-called 'rubble-masonry'), others have dressed stones that fit closely together and require less mortar and pointing. Look out also for other dressed stonework, such as blocks of pink/red sandstone and pale limestone, used for such features as window sills, door posts and lintels. Some of these are smooth but many are 'rusticated' – finished with smooth borders and a deliberately rough central area.

Significantly, South Road was developed southwards from the original town centre to connect with the new railways at Kirkby Stephen East Station (the Stainmore Railway, opened in August 1861) and Kirkby Stephen West Station (the Settle-Carlisle Railway, opened in May 1876). These Victorian-era houses were also built from Stenkrith Brockram, but a variety of materials have been used for the front walls. Red brick, white brick, glazed brick, and cut sandstone or limestone blocks may reflect a new affluence brought by the railways and a desire to 'stand out from' the local material, a phenomenon that can be seen again in the grander buildings in the centre of town. The new railways also enabled exotic materials to be transported more efficiently and cheaply across the country.

Approaching town – the 'Old Court House' of 1887 (**Waypoint 14**) is built of Stenkrith Brockram, as are the façades of the Wesleyan Centenary Chapel of 1839 (**Waypoint 15**) and the adjacent Wesleyan Sunday School (1879). Inspection reveals that the side walls of the Centenary Chapel were constructed using what appears to be random mixture of Stenkrith Brockram, sandstone and limestone; apparently any material that came to hand.

When walking around the centre of Kirkby Stephen look at the buildings and try to determine their relative age from the building materials used, noting that Stenkrith Brockram features in a large proportion of the older residential properties, the converted barns and the coach-houses. Although most of the buildings and shops along Market Street are built of brockram, many have been rendered or pebble-dashed and painted so the brockram only peeps out beside shop-window frames, or where the render or paint have flaked-off.

The centre of Kirkby Stephen, which was designated a 'Conservation Area' in 1976, contains many Grade II listed buildings[3]. These include the old Grammar School of 1566 (now the Library and Local Links **Waypoint 16**) and 17th century Frank's Bridge (**Waypoint 17**). Barclays Bank, 1903, (**Waypoint 18**), formerly Martins Bank, is faced with ashlar (a type of masonry that consists of finely dressed stones of the same shape, size, and texture laid in parallel 'courses' and bound with cement or lime mortar), although the sides are brockram. The War Memorial, 1920, (**Waypoint 19**) in Market Square is carved from Lazonby sandstone.[3]

Kirkby Stephen Parish Church (**Waypoint 20**) is known as the 'Cathedral of the Dales' and makes a fitting end to this short building stone tour. The church, which was founded around 1230, is built primarily of Penrith Sandstone, but several phases of building can be observed from the different materials used. The church tower was built in the early 16th century, the chancel and east chapels were rebuilt between 1847–51, while the nave and aisles were rebuilt between 1871–74. Particularly distinctive is the brockram eastern end. Finally, step inside the church to view the important collection of Saxon and Viking carved stones, mostly discovered in 1847 when the church was rebuilt.[4]

| **Fig. 1a** Close-up view of brockram showing assorted sizes of angular limestone fragments cemented by calcium carbonate. | **Fig. 1b** Nateby Road Bridge: rectangular brockram blocks in the abutments and sandstone blocks forming the arch. |

| **Fig. 1c** Drystone wall on Station Road built mainly of Stenkrith Brockram with limestone (upper RH) & sandstone (lower LH). | **Fig. 1d** Buildings along South Road: the former Westmorland Farmers Building built of brockram. |

Fig. 1 Some features along the Stenkrith Brockram Walk (photographs by Raynor Shaw)

SOURCES

[1] https://en.wikipedia.org/wiki/Breccia

[2] Brockram Breccia in: *Strategic Stone Study: A Building Stone Atlas of Cumbria* (2013), published by English Heritage, page 9. Available at: https://www.cumbria.gov.uk/eLibrary/Content/Internet/538/755/1929/421 17103947.pdf

[3] https://en.wikipedia.org/wiki/Listed_buildings_in_Kirkby_Stephen

[4] *A Heritage in Stone: A Note on the Collection of Pre-conquest Carved Stones on Display in Kirkby Stephen Parish Church.* Text by Martin Holdgate, photographs by Alan Coates, published by Kirkby Stephen Parochial Church Council.

PAUPERISM AND POOR-RELIEF: the Evolution of the Workhouse at Kirkby Stephen
Peter Lewis

*This article tells the story of the evolution of Kirkby Stephen's Workhouse, from its 18th century beginnings, not as a workhouse at all but a kind of factory, to its closure in 1930 and demolition in 1974. The author has used original sources where possible, although these are limited and occasionally contradictory. The text is illustrated (**Fig. 1** for example) with drawings by local artists, maps and photographs. However it is not only an account of a building, with some fascinating details revealed by the architectural sketches of Ken Martin, it is also a compelling and occasionally poignant summary of how the problem of acute poverty has been dealt with over the last 500 years.*

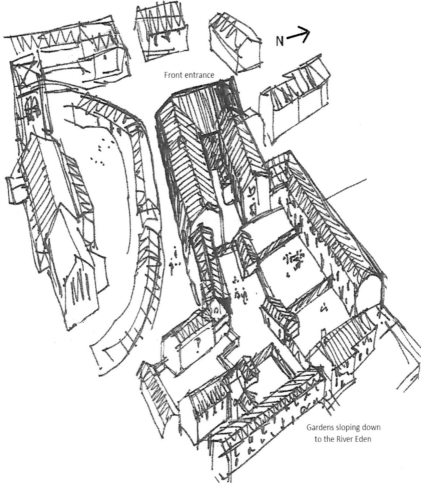

Fig. 1 How the Workhouse might have looked in the mid-late 19th century. Drawing courtesy of Ken Martin.

Prologue

Before the Dissolution of the Monasteries by Henry VIII, between 1536 and 1541, most poor relief was delivered by ecclesiastical institutions – the abbeys, convents, and priories. For the Kirkby Stephen catchment area these would have included the Priories at Appleby and Ravenstonedale, and the Abbey at Shap. The Dissolution had a truly devastating effect on poor relief countrywide – 800 or more ecclesiastical institutions, the main source of charity for the old and infirm, vanished virtually overnight. The provision of alms came to an abrupt end, and many almshouses were closed. This left the elderly, the sick, and the genuinely poor without support or accommodation for several decades, apart from the charity of their local communities.

There were other complications. From around 1500 to 1650 the population of England doubled to about 5 million people, creating many more mouths to feed. With a plentiful food supply this would not perhaps have presented such a problem, but there were disastrous harvest failures between 1594 and 1597, the cost of grain escalated beyond the means of most people, and real wages failed to keep up with food prices. The nation's fairly continuous and expensive international warfare (notably the Nine Years War with Ireland) added extra financial burdens. As a result poverty developed on a new and previously unseen scale, occasionally resulting in food riots.

As ever in times of poverty, then as now, there was an inevitable polarisation between the well-off (in particular the locally powerful yeoman farmers) and a significant part of the rest of the population, the 'ragged' people, the mass of the poor. Some commentators of the period judged the tensions of the Elizabethan 1590s to be a time of social crisis. The 'leaders' of society at the time (MPs, borough officials, parish constables, churchwardens and others) would have become increasingly aware of the pressure that this widespread poverty placed on the limited poor relief systems of towns such as Kirkby Stephen. Gradually the view formed that relieving the poor might be best managed by local parish authorities rather than by churches, charities, or community good will. A number of Acts of Parliament reflected this growing belief.

Poor Relief and the Law

This section summarises some of the relevant Acts of Parliament which attempted to address the thorny issue of poor relief. Their most essential details are listed in chronological order, commencing with 1552.

The Acts from which they are derived are listed in Appendix 1.

1. 1552 and 1572: a local property tax (the poor rate) levied on the property of the rate-paying wealthier members of the community, was proposed in order to raise funds to relieve the 'aged, poor, impotent, and decayed person'.

2. 1576: city, town, and other local authorities had to purchase materials for the able-bodied poor to work with so that they could earn a living. Materials included wool, hemp, and flax. The basic idea was to deprive the able-bodied poor of any excuse not to work so that all of them, especially the supposed 'malingerers', were obliged to work in order to earn a living.

3. 1597: Overseers of the Poor were to be appointed by every parish. Their role was:

- to collect the poor rate, and distribute poor-relief to those deemed in need. At first poor relief was usually given as 'outdoor' relief in the form of money, food, or other basic necessities;

- to find work for the able-bodied and provide them with the materials needed to do so;

- to set up parish houses, known as 'Houses of Dwelling' for those paupers who, for one reason or other, were unable to work to support themselves and so became destitute as a consequence.

4. 1601: able-bodied paupers who refused to work were liable to be sent to a House of Correction.

5. 1601: parishes became the administrative units responsible for poor relief. Under what came to be known as the Old Poor Law, parishes such as Kirkby Stephen were made legally responsible for their paupers, including those who were too ill, too young, or too elderly to work. The cost of poor relief was still to met by the Poor Rate.

6. 1662: the aim of this Act was to establish the parish to which a person belonged – where they were born, their place of settlement. This clarified which parish was responsible for providing someone with poor relief

when it was needed. Each person had to have a Settlement Certificate as identification and take it with them if they moved away from their home parish. If such a person needed poor relief then her/his home parish had to pay for the removal costs from host parish back to home parish. Host parishes had the right to remove newcomers, forcibly if necessary, within 40 days of arrival if it transpired that they would be a charge on the parish. Predictably, this legislation caused great hardship to migrant workers and their families.

7. 1723: with the passing of Knatchbull's Act, parishes were allowed to set up workhouses, either singly or in partnership with their neighbouring parishes.

8. 1782: the 'Workhouse Test' was introduced with the passing of what came to be known as Gilbert's Act. The intention was to use the offer of a place in the workhouse as a test of the motives of those applying for poor relief. It was intended as a test of genuine destitution and, for it to work properly, conditions in a workhouse had to be worse than the conditions a common labourer encountered outside. With this ideology, relief should only be given to those paupers who were sufficiently desperate, because of their poverty, to tolerate the deliberately hard regime of the workhouse. The idea was that many of the poor would be deterred from accepting poor relief in the workhouse, hence the notion of the deterrent workhouse.

9. 1782: Gilbert's Act also enabled neighbouring parishes, if they chose, to combine forces to form groups or 'unions' in order to set up a joint workhouse. Joint workhouses were intended to deliver poor relief on a larger scale than was previously possible. Membership of such unions was limited to parishes lying within a 10-mile radius of one another. Kirkby Stephen's Gilbert Union Workhouse was established in 1818 and, like all the others in the country, was:

- administered by a Board of Guardians, one Guardian for each parish involved;
- intended only for the old, the sick, the infirm, and for orphan children;
- to be a deterrent to the able-bodied but to provide a safety net of sorts for 'proper' paupers. Able-bodied paupers were not to be admitted to a Gilbert Workhouse but had to be found work near to their homes.

At various times there was one Gilbert Union Workhouse in Cumberland (Whitehaven), and four in Westmorland (Eamont Bridge, Kirkby Lonsdale, Kirkby Stephen and Milnthorpe).

10. 1819: Vestry Committees were enabled to appoint a small committee of 'substantial householders', known as the Select Vestry, to scrutinise the operation of its poor relief administration. This Act allowed ratepayers a greater say in such matters as how the poor rates were collected and distributed, and in what form they were given.

11. 1834: the New Poor Law was passed. The Act was compulsory, creating a national, centrally controlled system of poor relief with uniform rules to guide it. Its main provisions were:

- the system was based on groups of parishes and paid for out of the local poor rate;

- overall control was centralised in the form of a new authority called the Poor Law Commission (PLC) and its Commissioners;

- new administrative regions called Poor Law Unions were created. Kirkby Stephen and its local parishes came within the East Ward Union;

- each Union was expected to provide a workhouse which operated on the basis of the 'workhouse test'. It was intended that this test should be rigorously applied;

- each Union was still to be managed by a Board of Guardians elected by local ratepayers, although larger participating parishes could have more than one member;

- the new Poor Law Union Workhouses were the only form of relief available to able-bodied paupers and their families. Anyone receiving poor relief had to actually live in the Workhouse, although occasionally some were still considered 'deserving' of out-relief. They would have included cases of 'sudden and urgent necessity', newly widowed women, and accidental injuries;

- in return for poor relief in a workhouse, paupers had to cope with a number of demanding and unpleasant features: the segregation of males, females, and age groups; a long working day; hard, tedious, repetitive work (stone-breaking and arduous physical labour for men, teasing oakum for women); sacrificing personal liberty; living in an enclosed world cut off from the outside; strict discipline guided by a detailed system of rules and regulations.

The earlier versions of workhouses, often called poorhouses or houses of industry, were establishments in which, by and large, worthwhile work was done by able-bodied paupers. This might have involved, for example, combing wool, dressing flax and hemp, working with iron or wood, weaving flax for home use, and so on. Broadly speaking, these workhouses seem to have been more akin to non-residential workshops, a place where able-bodied paupers could work and earn money. Until the early 1800s the indigent, sick, young and elderly would still have received out-relief. Basically, poor relief during this period involved providing the means of working for the able-bodied together with out-relief (benefits in kind) for those who were unable to work.

However, there was no unified system of Poor Law administration until the New Poor Law was passed in 1834. Until then the attitudes and beliefs of the poor law authorities had varied across Cumberland and Westmorland. Consequently, in the absence of any binding guidelines from Parliament, the nature of the workhouses and poorhouses controlled by the local authorities differed markedly. Ultimately, the character of each of these houses differed according to the needs of different local communities. At a minimum estimate there were 46 workhouses and poorhouses of one type or another in Cumberland and Westmorland under the Old Poor Law, many being small unsupervised poorhouses with only a handful of inmates in each. Within this context there is no reason to think that Kirkby Stephen was different from any of the other rural townships at the time, where the workhouses/poorhouses would have been small, and were simply buildings adapted from a single or row of cottages where work was provided for the able-bodied pauper.

With specific reference to Kirkby Stephen, there are two primary sources of information about what has traditionally been considered as the town's original Poorhouse at Town Head. The first concerns Fawcett's drawing of the building, which he labelled the 'OLD POORHOUSE 1817'. The second stems from a study of the 17th and 18th century manorial records in which, among the rentals in Kirkby Stephen, were a dyehouse, a bakery, and a workhouse or poorhouse. The latter would most likely have been a workshop, possibly for weaving. On balance, whether it is preferable to call it a workshop, workhouse, poorhouse, or house of industry, it is probable that there was a poor relief facility of some kind based in what is now High Street. The old Town Head Cottages, now 87-88 High Street, have survived (**Fig. 2**).

Fig. 2 Town Head Cottages, Kirkby Stephen. Drawing courtesy of Ann Sandell.

Over time, however, it became apparent that the cost of out-relief was becoming increasingly expensive. The view gradually developed that the best way to keep down the overall cost was to establish larger and more formal workhouses. Furthermore, a shift in ideology was taking place that resulted in views on poor relief changing from 'relief of destitution' to 'deterrence of idleness'. This development had no sympathy whatsoever for people who struggled to look after themselves, such as abandoned mothers, illegitimate or abandoned children, widows and their families, 'idiots' and 'lunatics', or those incapacitated by age, illness, or injury.

The Manufactory – Forerunner of the New Workhouse
The site immediately to the north of the Parish Church, traditionally known as The Green, is understood by many to have been the original drovers' rest and possibly the early market centre of the town. It was there that the main workhouse was eventually built. A number of conveyances and other documents exist from late 1747 to 1810 that

repeatedly mention a 'factory' or 'manufactory' associated with that site, although none feature the terms poorhouse or workhouse. The contents of those documents, shown in italics, include:

- 12.10.1747: *Thomas Pearson on the surrender of John Harrison admitted to a tenement part of what is now the Factory*;

- 2.10.1749: *Elizabeth Hindmore sister [...] at law of Jonathan Hindmore admitted to the remainder of what is now the Factory along with other premises*;

- 19.10.1773: *Thomas Pearson [...] Factory*.

It is possible that the first Manufactory, most probably built during the mid-to-late 18th century, incorporated a fairly sophisticated residential town house. Photographs taken before the structure's demolition in 1974 indicate that many of the internal features of the northernmost building were more ornate and elaborate than would be expected for just a factory – as shown in **Fig. 3** of the first floor landing window, based on an early photograph. The second drawing, **(Fig. 4)** based on an architectural analysis, suggests how the residence might have looked when viewed from the main entrance in the west, with the factory wing (to the right) probably taking up the entire southern aspect of the building complex.

Fig. 3 First floor landing window
Drawing courtesy of Ken Martin

Fig. 4 How the residence might have looked
Drawing courtesy of Ken Martin

The 1700s was a period when genuine poverty had assumed alarming proportions. The social classes were divided between the rich, who were expected to pay the poor rates, and the poor who needed relief from their poverty. In a debate that echoes down the ages, the destitute poor were considered to be poverty-stricken by circumstances beyond their control (such as failed harvests or widespread unemployment), as a fundamental necessity for the economic system to operate, or as a life-style choice.

According to the available information, the creation of a Gilbert's Union Workhouse in Kirkby Stephen was not considered until the early 1800s, located on the site of the Manufactory described above. Until then the records continued to describe nothing more than a factory. For example:

- 14.10.1791: *William Crawford* [...] *Factory*;

- 6.12.1793: *Thomas Perceval* [...] *Factory*.

One obvious implication of the documents dating from October 1747 is that some sort of factory existed on the roughly triangular site a short distance to the north of the Parish Church. Some later written sources suggest that, about 1799, a cotton mill had been housed in quite a large building erected on the site by Messrs Graves, Lane & Co. The name 'Graves, Lane & Co' could not be located in the archive records, although the enterprise has been described as having become bankrupt in 1807. The main Kirkby Stephen industry during this period was in textiles and woollens, especially the making of hand-knitted stockings. It is not at all clear if this Manufactory had any function with regard to poor relief and, in the absence of information to the contrary, it is reasonable to conclude that the town's old Poorhouse was still in some way serving this purpose.

Other sources suggest that, about 1790, an entrepreneur from Manchester bought the ground with a view to establishing a mill. The enterprise initially seems to have been for spinning only, possibly driven by horse-power. This project seems to have failed quite rapidly, with the premises and equipment subsequently passing through several hands. For example, a conveyance dated 2nd March 1803 indicated that one Joseph Dent sold the property to *George Dickinson (late of Manchester, now of Kirkby Stephen, manufacturer). Premises, messuage* [a dwelling, possibly with land and outbuildings assigned to its use], *tenement or dwelling house where Thomas Pearson family lived and Joseph Dent lately lived with all warehouses, barns, byres, stables, and courthouses belonging and adjoining on north side of churchyard with garden and orchard and appats in town of Kirkby Stephen* [...] *for £292.* If the mill had ever operated there would have been spinning, weaving and 'wet' work (i.e. dyeing), which would have involved tentering, and possibly a tenterfield for wool on the River Eden in the Stenkrith area. It is unlikely that there had been a successful cotton industry in the Kirkby Stephen area during the 18th or 19th centuries due, in large part, to its relative isolation and poor transport links.

From 1807 onwards there were several recorded dealings with regard to the site and its premises. While there are occasional inconsistencies in some of the documented dates, the most significant developments include the following:

- in 1807 the properties were bought by John Dand *of the City of Carlisle* [...] *banker and manufacturer*;

- at some point Dand opened a bank on the site but was declared bankrupt in 1808;

- the properties were subsequently sold in 1809 to Richard Binks. The memorandum of sale included *looms, material of looms, frames for dressing cotton warps, branches, stoves, boilers, drums, shafts* [balers] *at Stenkrith* [situated at the opposite end of town to the Manufactory];

- it seems likely that the site also housed a school. Under the headmastership of Richard Aislabie, it was known as either 'the Classical and Commercial Academy, Eden Hall', or 'the Eden Hall Seminary of Education for Boys'. While difficult to be certain, it is possible that the school was operational until around 1815, possibly as late as 1818. Aislabie died on 11th November 1818. Binks was the younger brother of Richard Aislabie's mother Martha, and therefore was Aislabie's uncle.

Again, there is nothing in the available records to suggest that anything on the site, whether Manufactory, school, or bank, had any connection with poor relief. This situation changed in 1818.

Kirkby Stephen's Gilbert Workhouse

Under the terms of the 1782 Gilbert's Act (passed 36 years previously), on 14th November 1818 Binks sold all the relevant premises in his possession to Kirkby Stephen's Guardians of the Poor for £1500. The conveyance document read: *by virtue [...] of the directions of an Act of Parliament made and passed in the [?] year of the reign of his majesty King George III entitled "an Act for the better relief and employment of the Poor" of the other part WITNESSETH that for and [?] of the sum of One Thousand Five Hundred pounds to said Richard Binks.*

According to the indenture the premises included: *mess.* [messuage] *and vent* [?] *called the Manufactory consisting of dwelling house, school rooms, townhouse, chattles, coal-house, rooms called the banking house, bake house, pig-styles, shed and other buildings with yard and garden adjoining round all erections and buildings lately used as a manufactory all in occupation of John Nelson; also mess. cottage or dwelling house adjoining in occupation of Martha Storey and Joseph Mason – all on north side of church-yard in KS; and all fixtures and machinery. Consideration £1500.*

This new Gilbert's Union Workhouse in Kirkby Stephen involved the collaborative partnership of six parishes: Hartley, Kirkby Stephen, Mallerstang, Nateby, Soulby, and Winton. Unfortunately, the County Archives hold only limited catalogued information about the Workhouse from 1818 to 1836. What is available indicates the following:

- in 1827 workhouse premises, in part or whole, were let to John Henry Wilson, a Manchester manufacturer, for the production of silk and cotton goods. The intention had been to employ the paupers profitably in weaving. In 1839, however, the Assistant Poor Law Commissioner, Mr Voules, reported that the business had collapsed because of *the great fluctuations in pauperism [...] the looms* [were] *dilapidated and deserted [...] and paupers of both sexes lounging in promiscuous intercourse in every part of the building and yards.* In any event, over time the view developed that weaving was not a sufficiently demanding labour test and by 1842 stone breaking had replaced weaving as the main male pauper employment;

- in 1829 Edward Ewbank was the Governor and Assistant Overseer of the Gilbert's Workhouse;

- from the 1831 Census, the average annual poor-rate expenditure for the period 1834 to 1836 was £5,647 7s 9d. That is, 7s 9d per head of population.

In summary, from 1818 until 1836 there had been a Gilbert's Poor Law Union of six local parishes, with Kirkby Stephen hosting a Workhouse established under the terms of the 1782 Act.

The Era of the New Poor Law
In 1834, the Elizabethan Old Poor Law was superseded by what, unsurprisingly, came to be known as the New Poor Law. Across the country, the 1500 or so parishes in England and Wales had to be divided into new administrative units called 'Poor Law Unions', usually combinations of 20 to 30 parishes. Of the two counties:

- Cumberland was divided into 9 such Unions: Alston, Bootle, Brampton, Carlisle, Cockermouth, Long Town, Penrith, Whitehaven, and Wigton.

- and Westmorland into 3 Unions: East Ward Union, Kendal, and West Ward Union. The Workhouse in Kirkby Stephen was based in the East Ward Union.

Under the terms of the New Poor Law Westmorland's East Ward Poor Law Union formally came into being on 31st October 1836. What had been the Kirkby Stephen Gilbert Union Workhouse became the Workhouse for the new East Ward Poor Law Union, taking over its associated properties. Each new Poor Law Union was to be run by a Board of Guardians who were elected at the start of April each year by the ratepayers in each union parish.

The Guardians of the new East Ward Union met for the first time at the Court House, Appleby, on 1st November 1836. It was agreed that they should meet weekly, on Saturdays, alternating between Appleby Town Hall and the Workhouse in Kirkby Stephen. The 30 parishes (with spellings as recorded in the minutes and ledgers) listed as members of the new Union at that first meeting were: Asby; the Broughs; Brough Sowerby; Crosby Garrett; Dufton; Great Musgrave; Hartley; Hillbeck; Kaber; Kirkby Stephen; Kirkby Thore; Little Musgrave; Mallerstang; Marton; Milburne; Nateby; Newbiggin; Ormside; Orton; Ravonstonedale;

St. Lawrence, Appleby; St. Michael, Bongate; Smardale; Soulby; Stainmore; Temple Sowerby; Wateby; Warcop; Wharton; and Winton.

In later records, the following parishes were also recorded: Crackenthorpe (from 1894); Murton (1894); Hilton; Colby (1894); Drybeck, Hoff (1894); and Tebay (1897).

By and large, the formation of the East Ward Union seems to have taken place without incident. Some resistance came from *the isolated parish of Ravenstonedale* which pleaded for a second Guardian to represent its interests on the Board of Governors because its isolation made their attendance difficult. Also, in May 1837, the ratepayers of Ravenstonedale petitioned Parliament against the New Poor Law, claiming it was inapplicable to rural areas. Nothing came of either request.

At a subsequent meeting of the Guardians, held on 24th December 1836, Thomas Parkinson was appointed the new Master of the Workhouse: *Mr Thomas Parkinson of Kirkby Lonsdale was appointed to the situation of Master of the workhouse at a salary of £30 pa.* [...] *Mrs Mary Parkinson […] to the situation of Matron at a salary of £15 pa.* The couple were Master and Matron from 1836 to 1846.

Thus from November 1836 the East Ward Poor Law Union took over the old Gilbert Workhouse premises, (see **Fig. 5** for the Tithe Map). However, it is not entirely clear when the purchase of the site was actually completed, as the following minutes reveal:

- 12th November, 1836: a committee was formed *for the purpose of inspecting the Workhouse at Kirkby Stephen to ascertain its capabilities for the reception of the Paupers of the East Ward Union, and that they be further empowered to enter into a negotiation with the Trustees* [of the township of Kirkby Stephen] *in whom the said premises are vested with a view either to rent or purchase the same and report thereon;*

- 3rd December, 1836: the committee *came to the determination that £800 was a fair value for them* [the premises] *and that such should be offered for the same on behalf of the Union.*

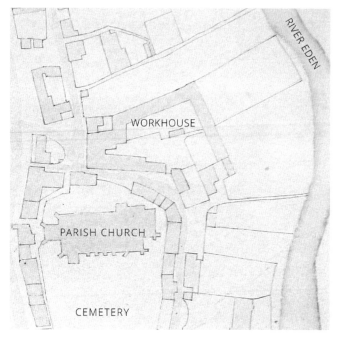

Fig. 5 1839 Tithe Map of Kirkby Stephen, showing position
of the Workhouse and Parish Church house and Parish Church.

However, the township wanted £1000 for its property and refused the
offer. The issue was left to one of the Poor Law Commissioners (W J
Voules) to fix the price and in December 1836 he decided that £850 was a
suitable price for the *Workhouse at Kirkby Stephen including the fixtures*.
The transaction was eventually completed on 1st January 1840 when
*£850 paid by Guardians of the Poor of East Ward Union to the Treasurer
of the Union, re the sale of certain premises belonging to the township of
Kikby Stephen.*

To Build or Not to Build A New Workhouse
From the earliest days of the creation of the East Ward Poor Law Union
there was debate over how to provide a workhouse which would meet the
demands of the New Poor Law. Ultimately it was a choice between:

• whether to enlarge and adapt the existing buildings;

• or to start afresh and build a new 'bespoke' workhouse.

60

This debate was conducted primarily between the central government's Poor Law Commissioners (who wanted a new building), and the local Guardians (who did not). Only three of the twelve Poor Law Unions in Cumberland & Westmorland erected new workhouses. The East Ward Union was not one of them.

One of the main problems confronting most if not all Guardians was that many of the existing Gilbert Union buildings, including Kirkby Stephen's, were of poor quality and were often cramped, badly ventilated, and with poor sanitation. Matters were further complicated by the legal requirement of the Act that Workhouse inmates should be segregated by age and gender, a demand that was, to a very large extent, beyond the capabilities of many existing workhouses. The segregation, or 'classification', was intended to be into seven categories:

    i.   aged or infirm males;
    ii.   able-bodied men and youths older than 13 (from 1842 this changed to older than 15);
    iii.   youths and boys older than 7 but younger than 13 (from 1842, younger than 15);
    iv.   females who were infirm through age or other causes
    v.   able-bodied women and girls older than 16 (from 1842, older than 15);
    vi.   girls older than 7 but younger than 16 (from 1842, younger than 15);
    vii.   children under the age of 7.

Clearly dispute of one sort or another was inevitable. On the one hand, the Poor Law Commissioners attempted to persuade the Governors to build new bespoke workhouses or, at the very least, to make substantial improvements to the existing workhouses. On the other hand, the 'real' authority lay locally with the Guardians, who had costs firmly in mind. While the Poor Law Commissioners could veto any plans put to them, the initiative for either developing existing facilities or building a new workhouse lay firmly with the Guardians.

Cost was always going to be an issue in these matters. In rural unions the overwhelming proportion of Guardians were small-to-medium landowners and farmers who were suffering economic hardships during the general agricultural depression, caused in part by the general fall in the price of agricultural produce following the Napoleonic wars. The

Guardians were the ones who would invariably have had to foot any bill to build a new workhouse.

As a consequence, most Boards of Guardians chose to patch up existing workhouses rather than undertake the expense of costly new buildings. Such was the case with the East Ward Union where the Guardians decided that it was preferable to develop what they already had rather than to build a new Workhouse. At one point the Kirkby Stephen Guardians believed that £50 spent on the existing Workhouse would deal with any significant deficiencies. The Guardians' view was summed up in their meeting held on 24th December 1836: *The Committee are of the opinion that the different rooms it* [the old Gilbert Union Workhouse] *contains affords comfortable accommodation for 56 persons. Also of the opinion that a dormitory capable of containing 18 double beds may at a trifling expense be made in the upper floor of the long room, thus making sleeping accommodation for 92 persons.*

Having agreed to redevelop what they already had, the Guardians set out to buy additional properties to add to the Workhouse 'portfolio':

- 28th May 1838: *Thomas Fawcett of Dent, gentleman, sold to EWU Guardians, a housestead and garden, Back Street, Kirkby Stephen, for £38*;

- 19th May 1840: *From Mr Simpson, for £93, a housestead in Kirkby Stephen, converted into a schoolhouse by the Guardians*;

- 19th May 1840: *from Mr Abraham Simpson to Guardians of the East Ward Union Westmorland, a Housestead in Kirkby Stephen £93, converted into schoolhouse by Guardians*

As it turned out the East Ward Union Workhouse required extensive alterations to meet the demands of classification. The expense of purchasing additional properties and of alterations and refurbishment to accommodate 100 inmates came to around £2,000. Alterations were still in progress 2 years after the East Ward Union was formed and effective classification remained incomplete. This fact was brought home to the Guardians when William C. (pauper) made Jane S. (a fellow pauper) pregnant, highlighting the inadequacies of the institution's segregation.

At some point during the early-to-mid 19th century a second floor was added to the original Georgian town house, to both extend the accommodation for the Master and his family and to provide additional servants' quarters. The factory part of the structure was also modified to create two storeys, with a bakery on the ground floor below an 8-bed female sick ward (see **Fig. 8**), although the resulting monopitch design added little to the aesthetic quality of the buildings (see **Fig. 6**; **Fig. 7**; **Fig. 9**).

The front of the modified workhouse
Fig. 6 Drawing courtesy of Ken Martin.   **Fig. 7** Photograph (source unknown)

Fig. 8 Eight-bed female sick ward.   **Fig. 9** View of the south-facing 'factory' wing
Drawing courtesy of Ken Martin.   Drawing courtesy of Ken Martin.

The care of children was a particular concern. The system of classification was intended to separate impressionable children from the contaminating influence of adult inmates because, it was believed, pauper adults might have an evil influence on pauper children. The logic was that pauper children could not be freed (emancipated) from pauperism if they were allowed to associate with inappropriate persons. In October 1859 T B Browne, a workhouse school inspector, wrote of Harraby Hill Workhouse in Carlisle: *the poor law inspector* [N E Hurst or Hirst] *has invited my attention to the fact that women, the mothers of bastard children, are constantly permitted to work with the girls in the workhouse* [...] *the effects of such association are very injurious to the girls.*

Predictably perhaps the matter did not end there and the issue of whether or not to build a new workhouse rumbled on. Jumping ahead in time, in the early 1860s the Poor Law Board tried again to persuade the Guardians of the necessity to construct a new workhouse but, as before, they were met by a determined Board of Guardians who presented a new plan to modify the old and rambling existing building. This was despite a report in 1866 that described the workhouse as *an old and dilapidated building with very low rooms, and where the classification* [of inmates] *and arrangements were very imperfect.*

The differences in opinion were so great that there were even suggestions that the East Ward and West Ward Unions should combine to build and share a new workhouse. Opinions vacillated as the debate wore on:

- 10th Feb 1862: letter from Reverend Simpson of the West Ward Union to the East Ward, suggesting that the two unions combine to form a single workhouse. The East Ward's response was blunt and to the point – *the proposal is not entertained*;

- 21st April 1862: *The* [East Ward Union] *committee met for the purpose of further considering the* [...] *matter* [...] *Thoughts even strayed to the possibility of the West and East Ward Unions sharing a new joint workhouse* [...];

- 1st February 1873: letter from the East Ward Clerk to the West Ward Union: *it would be a great saving expense to the advantage of the East and West Wards if these two unions were combined with one common workhouse*;

- 12th March 1873: the East Ward Union Guardians *agreed a deputation to meet with the West Ward Union* to discuss this matter further;

- 18th March 1873: the idea was finally dropped.

The result of a decade of discussion was that a new workhouse in Kirkby Stephen was never built, and any thoughts of a joint Union Workhouse with the West Ward Union were summarily dismissed. Eventually, in 1877, a new West Ward Union Workhouse was built in Shap to replace the old Gilbert's Union Workhouse in Eamont Bridge.

How Was the East Ward Union Workhouse Organised?

From an examination of various maps, plans, surveys and witness reports, it is reasonable to conclude that the institution would have been organised along the following lines (see **Fig. 10**).

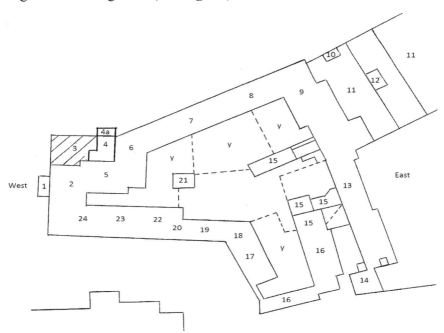

Fig. 10 Numbered plan, showing lay-out.

1:      Front entrance.
2:      Ground floor: entrance hall; Master's office; boardroom; parlour; cloakroom; cellar; 2 pantries; larder; bread store; large cooking kitchen; wash house;
        First floor: 2 Master's bedrooms; Matron's bedroom; bathroom; lavatory and WC; Matron's sewing room; maternity bedroom; clothing store;
        Second floor: 4 bedrooms; 2 box rooms (possibly staff living quarters);
3:      Boiler man's house;
4:      Boiler man's yard;
4a: Possible site of boiler house and chimney;
5:      Kitchen; sewing room;
6:      Clothing store; two 6-bed female bedrooms;
7:      Inmates dining hall; able-bodied female day-room and nursery; able-bodied male day-room; 8-bed male bedroom;
8:      Lean-to wash-room; storehouse;
9:      Male sick ward (14 beds); male dormitory (14 beds); small male dormitory (3 beds);
10:     Greenhouse;
11:     Garden;
12:     Coal house;
13:     Men's sick ward; male vagrants casual ward; 11-bed infectious casual ward;
14:     Porter's office and bedroom;
15:     Privvies; WCs; bathroom;
16:     Lean-to boiler house; sticks; logs; stone crushing/breaking shed; coal shed;
17:     Female casual ward;
18:     Female receiving ward; lean-to WC;
19:     Paupers' entrance; porter's lodge/room;
20:     Male receiving ward;
21:     Mortuary;
22:     Workshops; porter's store; scullery; bedding stores;
23:     Two bathrooms; ironing room; laundry; store room; coal house; two 6-bed female bedrooms;
24:     Bakery; 8-bed female sick ward;
Y: Yards.

This plan suggests that the East Ward Union Guardians had done their best to comply with the demands of the New Poor Law, although there were certainly some omissions. Most notable is what seems to be a lack of provision for the segregation of children from adults. Also a school room must have been present somewhere on site as evidenced by the number of children the Workhouse had to cater for over the years, and the existence of teacher and school records and reports.

Who Were the Workhouse Inmates?
Even a cursory analysis of the Census Returns reveals that, over the years, the East Ward Union Workhouse inmates reflected society at large, certainly the poorer classes, the paupers coming from different walks of life, ages, and circumstances.

While the local authorities undoubtedly appreciated the Workhouse Test as a means of testing destitution, there is little evidence to suggest that they made a determined effort to adopt this principle in the *modus operandi* of the Workhouse. On the one hand there had to be a 'deterrent' Workhouse for the able-bodied destitute, but on the other the authorities were required to provided an institution geared towards the caring for pauper children and their education; the old and disabled; the mentally ill and 'weak minded'; unmarried mothers and their children; and the sick. The East Ward Union Workhouse did, at one time or another, try to meet the needs of all these pauper groups. Indeed, as the decades passed, the notion of the deterrent Workhouse 'withered on the vine' and increasingly the Workhouse became an institution more of care than deterrence. In many ways it anticipated the modern welfare state.

Age groups as per New Poor Law classification	1841	1851	1861	1871	1881	1891	1901	1911
Boys up to 6	10	17	9	1	5	5	2	0
Girls up to 6	10	9	13	6	5	6	1	1
Boys 7-12	11	17	8	7	4	3	0	0
Girls 7-15	6	9	7	5	3	3	0	0
Males 13-59	15	9	20	13	8	11	6	11
Females 16-59	19	36	21	8	8	7	7	10
Males 60+	21	7	12	16	8	6	28	22
Females 60+	12	8	7	4	1	1	2	6
Prob number of unmarried femailes	-	9	5	3	2	3	1	1
and children	-	19	8	8	3	7	1	1
Prob. number of widows	-	8	3	1	2	2	0	0
and children	-	21	9	3	5	2	0	0
Unaccompanied children	12	9	9	5	2	6	2	0
No. of children	37	52	37	19	17	17	3	1
No. of cripples	1	0	0	0	0	0	0	1
No. imbeciles	6	11	0	3	0	0	0	15
No. of lunatics	1	1	0	1	0	0	0	0
Total number of inmates	**104**	**112**	**97**	**60**	**42**	**42**	**46**	**50**

Fig. 11 Table of inmates' categories at 8 census points. Some inmates are recorded in more than one category. The final row gives the actual total number of inmates residing in the workhouse at the census points.

Occupation	1841	1851	1861	1871	1881	1891	1901	1911
Agric lab.	1	2	0	3	-	-	4	12
Blacksmith	1	2	0	0	-	-	0	0
Bdg lab.	0	1	0	1	-	-	0	1
Butcher	3	0	1	0	-	-	0	0
Carpenter	0	0	0	0	-	-	1	2
Carter	0	0	0	1	-	-	0	0
Chairmaker	0	0	1	0	-	-	0	0
Charwoman	4	2	4	0	-	-	0	2
Clogger	0	0	0	1	-	-	0	0
Cook	0	0	0	0	-	-	0	1
Cordwainer	1	0	0	1	-	-	0	0
Spinner	0	1	1	0	-	-	0	0
Dressmaker	1	1	2	0	-	-	0	0
Engine fitter	0	1	0	1	-	-	0	
Gen. lab	5	2	0	0	-	-	6	8
Servant	15	29	15	9	-	-	4	5
Hawker	0	1	1	0	-	-	2	2
House kpr.	4	1	0	0	-	-	5	1
Lodg. kpr	0	2	0	0	-	-	0	0
Miner	1	0	0	1	-	-	0	0
Rlwy lab.	0	0	16	15	-	-	0	0
Sawyer	0	2	0	0	-	-	0	0
Seamster	0	2	0	0	-	-	0	0
Shoe maker	3	1	0	0	-	-	0	1
Sol's clerk	0	0	0	0	-	-	1	0
Slater	1	0	0	0	-	-	0	2
Tailor	1	0	1	0	-	-	0	1
Weaver	4	4	0	2	-	-	0	1
Wool spinnr	3	0	0	1	-	-	0	0
Children	37	52	37	19	17	17	3	1baby
Vag./casual	4	1	0	0	0	0	16	0
Inmate total	104	112	97	60	42	42	46	50

Fig. 12 Table of inmates' occupations/categories at census points.

69

A full analysis of these figures (**Fig. 11** and **Fig. 12**) is beyond the scope of this article, although certain matters are evident.

- The consistently largest group, at least until 1901, was the number of children. Over the sixty-year Census period, the percentage of children in the Workhouse was 36, 46, 38, 32, 41, and 41. The figures fell to 7 and 2 for 1901 and 1911 respectively.

- The second largest group was men and women aged 60 years or more. As per the Census dates the percentages were 32, 13, 20, 33, 21, and 17, rising significantly to 65 and 56 in 1901 and 1911 respectively.

- Agricultural labourers peaked in 1911.

- Railway workers (navvies) only appeared, albeit in high numbers, in 1861 and 1871. While the figures for 1861 remain something of a mystery, navvies had been employed on the construction of the Settle & Carlisle railway for 7 years from 1869 to 1876. It is likely that the high 1871 Census figures for the Workhouse involved navvies admitted to the Workhouse Infirmary, reflecting either injuries incurred on the line or diseases such as smallpox and typhoid. Smallpox was prevalent during the summer and autumn of 1871, and typhus fever during early 1874. It is also likely that some of the injured had already been inmates of the Workhouse who had been 'subcontracted' to the railway company.

Who Were the Workhouse Masters and Matrons?

The East Ward Union Workhouse Master, appointed by the Board of Guardians, was responsible for the overall administration of the workhouse. The Matron (usually the Master's wife) was responsible for general house-keeping, and for all female inmates and children under 7. Unfortunately the records, notably the Guardians' minutes, tend to refer to the Masters and Matrons by title rather than by name, making accurate identification and dating difficult. What follows is based on the best available information but may contain some errors.

Edward Ewbank (1829-1836);
Thomas and Mary Parkinson (1836-1846);
John and Dorothy Askew (1846-1857);

John and Sarah Clark (1857-1874);
Andrew and Elizabeth Mackereth (1874-c1898);
Frederick and Mary Ann Harrison (c1901-1907);
Arthur Faulkner (1907-1910);
Robert and Margaret Atkinson (1910, possibly 1911);
John and Edith Ratcliffe (1910-1914);
Daniel and Annie Clarke (1914-1930).

What Other Workhouse Staff Were There?

There were other Workhouse staff in addition to the Master and Matron, both part- and full-time. Part-time staff included the Clerk, Treasurer, Auditor, Chaplain, and Medical Officers such as:

- Reverend Stephen Harrison, Chaplain, 1862;

- Medical Officers: Mr. G. Brydon; William Wilson; William Coltart; Mr. Dinnwoodie; George Spencer.

The East Ward Union Workhouse also had a complement of full-time staff, often referred to as indoor staff:

- Receiving Officers. They visited people who applied for assistance and assessed what relief, if any, should be given. For example:

  - 1844: John Bowman and Mr. Harding;
  - 1846: John again, along with John Idle;
  - 1871: Mr. Wilson and Mr. Dixon;

- Teachers: details are presented in the section below;

- Porters: invariably male, their job was to keep the gate; prevent unauthorised persons entering; record 'to-ings' and 'fro-ings'; receive all new admissions; inspect all items entering and leaving the Workhouse; search male paupers; lock all outer doors and take the keys to the Master; and help to preserve order in the Workhouse. Some of the porters were:

  1848: Thomas Mason.
  1871: Christopher Sanderson. On 18th January 1873, *The*

Master reported to the Board that Christopher Sanderson the workhouse porter was intoxicated on the evening of the 14th and that, on the following morning, he absented himself from his duties and has not since returned . Dismissed.

> 1873: Robert Railton.
> 25th April 1873: *Mr. Railton vacated his office without notice.*
> 1874: Peter Warburton.

- Nurses: 1874: Mary Thompson; Julia Warburton.
- Charwomen: 1873: Dickinson and Thompson.

Children and the Workhouse School

Children, arguably more than any other class of pauper, did not fit easily into the New Poor Law's notion of pauperism and deterrence. Only with difficulty could children have been considered responsible for becoming paupers. While some pauper children came with able-bodied parents who had been forced into the Workhouse, many had been either orphaned, deserted, or were illegitimate. In the 1850s children, this most blameless and vulnerable of groups, made up about 40% of the total workhouse population.

While there are no site plans to indicate where it might have been based in the premises, the Kirkby Stephen Workhouse would have contained a school room which enabled the pauper children to get a decent rudimentary education. The teachers concentrated on providing a basic standard in the 3 'Rs', and also taught geography and history.

Schooling began as early as 3 years of age and continued until the child left the Workhouse. In Kirkby Stephen, as in all Workhouse schools, a regular daily routine was followed, beginning with morning prayers at 7.00 am and ending with evening prayers and bed at 8.00 pm. The timetable incorporated periods for play and free time, and one day a week was set aside for recreation. Sunday was reserved for prayer, readings, and church services, emphasising the importance that the Guardians placed on moral and religious instruction.

For boys after 1850, emphasis was placed on industrial training. The Poor Law Board also pursued a policy of encouraging Guardians to purchase land adjoining the Workhouse, which would allow them to teach how to cultivate a garden ground and thereby learn husbandry. By the time boys had reached the age of 14 they were usually apprenticed to a trade. In rural areas this tended to involve entering the service of a local farmer as a farm servant, but many workhouses had the tradition of sending boys to sea or to join the army.

For girls, given the domestic routine of the workhouse, it was easier to find tasks such as *sewing, knitting, washing, 'getting up' linen, making bread, and the usual domestic occupations.* Nursing was morally more difficult as it involved girls mixing with other adult Workhouse inmates and so would have been *quite incompatible with their receiving proper instruction.*

More broadly the ideology behind the New Poor Law dictated that the life of pauper children had to be one of a small, closed existence, deliberately isolated from any contact with the outside world, fellow paupers and often even their parents. There is no doubt that Kirkby Stephen's Guardians found it difficult to comply with this, a view made easier by an Act of 1855 which made it legal for poor children and the children of out-door paupers to attend the Workhouse school.

However, this practice was contrary to the New Poor Law concept of the Workhouse as detached from the community, and many were against the mixing of children from inside and outside the Workhouse. Some argued that Workhouse schools were overcrowded, and that the admission of outsiders raised the danger of introducing infection into the Workhouse. With regard to Kirkby Stephen, on 19th November 1860, the Poor Law Inspector N. E. Hurst (or Hirst) suggested that *the itch* had been introduced into the Workhouse by out-door paupers attending the school. Exercising commendable independence, the Guardians chose instead to listen to the advice of the Inspector of Workhouse Schools, Edmund Woodhouse, and continued to admit outdoor paupers, so pursuing their aim of extending education to as many children as possible.

During the second half of the 19th century Workhouses, including Kirby Stephen's, increasingly sent their children out to local schools. Also in Kirkby Stephen, some time prior to 1877, a National Elementary Education school for boys was opened in the Temperance Hall (for 27 boys), girls joining them in 1870. On 2nd May 1877 the current Primary

School, built by the School Board, opened for business catering for all school age children. It is still in its original buildings.

The historical records contain these details of Kirkby Stephen's Workhouse schooling:

- 8th September 1837: *That William Curwen be appointed schoolmaster with a salary of 4s a week in addition to being allowed his diet in the house and that his children be allowed to remain in the workhouse for a fortnight*;

- 22nd September 1837: *That the Committee of Management be requested to take steps to provide a schoolmaster to teach the children in the workhouse*;

- 27th December 1839: *John Fothergill appointed schoolmaster.* He was there until at least January 1841;

- 18th December 1852: Mrs. Margaret Armstrong became the school mistress, followed by Ann Savage in 1862. Ann was still there on Oct 19th 1863;

- 4th December 1871: *Certificate of Proficiency First Division granted to Miss Bramley.*

What must have been particularly pleasing to all concerned with the children's education were these very positive school inspectors' reports:

- 11th August 1862: *Workhouse school. Read the following report of Mr T B Browne, one of Her Majesty's Inspectors of Schools after his visit to the workhouse school on 8th inst. 'The children in the school [...] a pleasing and creditable examination and appear to be very fairly taught. I am sorry to observe that the attendance of out-door children is so much smaller than it used to be'*;

- 20th November 1871: Report by HM Inspector of Union Schools, J R Mozley: *I have today examined the school. The children passed a very fair examination throughout. A little more attention should be paid to the rotation of numbers. There seemed to be a good tone among the children and a disposition to learn.*

The New Sick Ward

The development of a sick ward on the site reflected yet again the seemingly never-ending debate between the central authority in London (the Poor Law Board) and the East Ward Union Guardians about building a new Workhouse rather than adapting and extending the old, dilapidated premises:

- 24th March 1862: *Read letter from the Poor Law Board dated 20th March, inst., requesting to be informed what decision the Guardians had come to with the view to improve the accommodation for the sick and infectious cases*;

- 7th April 1862: *The Poor Law Board having again expressed their dissatisfaction with the accommodation in the workhouse for the sick and infectious cases, the Committee recommended that the plan proposed a short time ago for the erection of a sick ward be carried out by the Guardians*;

- 21st April 1862: *The committee met for the purpose of further considering the plan made […] for increasing the accommodation for the sick inmates of the workhouse. The committee, after maturely considering the plan made by Wm Close are of the opinion that it is the best that can be adopted in the existing workhouse of taking into consideration the present and probable prospective number of sick paupers. They are of the opinion that when completed the sick wards will be amply sufficient to meet the wants of the Union [...] Guardians to forward the plans to the Poor Law Board for their approval*;

- 19th May 1862: The Poor Law Board requested a rough sketch of the proposed plan;

- 5th July 1862: The Poor Law Board approved the plan but, not giving up, argued that a *much more advisable mode of providing the required accommodation would be by the erection of an entirely new workhouse*;

- 14th July 1862: *The Guardians are of the opinion that it is not necessary to erect an entirely new workhouse and that with the proposed additions to the present building it will be adequate*;

- 8th Sept 1862: *Resolved that the sum to be expended on the erection of the new sick wards at the Union workhouse shall not exceed the sum of £600.* The minutes also specified the contributions to be made by each member parish. The largest were committed from Appleby St. Lawrence (£98), Orton (£96), and Ravenstonedale (£69).

Tenders for the work were received in December 1862 and, in February 1863, the Board of Guardians accepted the offer of a loan of £300 at 4% interest from *Wm Richardson, Crosby Garrett* to help finance the building of the new sick wards. In the early 1860s a hospital was built on the East side of the Workhouse, and [it] *now forms a clean and salubrious resort for all kinds of sick patients […] it says, however, a good deal for the habits of frugality and independence of the poorer classes of this town that there has rarely been a hospital patient, except among the inmates of the Workhouse itself.*

Certainly the new sick wards were well equipped in comparison to the rest of the Workhouse, and proved to be a timely development because in 1871 there was a smallpox epidemic amongst railway workers in the East Ward Union. Indeed such was the demand for health care that the Guardians also provided a temporary fever hospital in Appleby.

The End of the Deterrent Workhouse Looms Into Sight
In general the Cumbrian workhouses did not seem to have subscribed to the concept of the deterrent workhouse and increasingly they evolved towards becoming institutions of care. Not exactly consistent with political orthodoxy of the time they became more 'caring', especially with regard to the well-being of the elderly and children, and to medical treatment and public health.

It is fair to say that the Boards of Guardians were never just deferential, obedient 'lap dogs' of central government. While there were exceptions, they and the workhouse Masters tended to take account of and were guided by local wishes and needs. Also, while trying to meet the overall demands of the New Poor Law, they attempted to provide firm but fair poor relief designed for their own specific communities. In doing so they seemed to be well aware of the paradox between 'proper objects of relief', the paupers they knew and lived amongst (particularly in fairly small communities such as Kirkby Stephen) and the concept of the deterrent workhouse, and interpreted the New Poor Law accordingly. Overall it seems that the Cumberland and Westmorland Boards of Guardians found it difficult to accept the political ideology of the New Poor Law system in its entirety and, as one commentator put it, *Guardians [...] by and large, [were] practical men who were more alive to the arguments of expedience than to abstract dogma.*

From the 1890s onwards, workhouses tended to become refuges for the aged and sick, remaining relatively unchanged until the 1920s. Nationally, the composition of the Board of Guardians also started to change. Women had never actually been barred from becoming Guardians, but it was not until 1875 (in Kensington) that the first female Guardian was elected, one Martha Merrington. By 1895 there were 839 female Guardians in the country but unfortunately none in Kirkby Stephen.

In 1919 the newly created Ministry of Health took over the administration of health and poor relief. The tragedy of WWI, followed by the general depression and 1926 miners' strike, put an almost intolerable strain on the system of poor relief. This eventually led to Neville Chamberlain, the Health Minister in the Conservative government of 1925, triggering changes culminating in the Local Government Act. This was passed on 27th March 1929 and came into effect on 1st April 1930.

The main consequences of this legislation were:

- on that date in 1930, 643 Boards of Guardians were abolished;

- their powers and responsibilities were transferred to local councils. For Kirkby Stephen this meant the County Council of Westmorland;

- local authorities gained the power to take over workhouse infirmaries as municipal hospitals;

- workhouses officially ceased to exist, 'morphing' into Public Assistance Institutions (PAI)

- the East Ward Union Workhouse duly became Eden House, PAI.

Showing commendable good humour, the about-to-expire East Ward Union Board of Guardians arranged a celebratory dinner to commemorate the *passing of the Guardians' duties, to be held as early as possible in April* [1930], *at a cost of no more than 5/- a head.* The newspaper report of that dinner, as humorous as one will ever come across under such circumstances, is recorded in its near entirety in Appendix 2.

Eden House PAI continued to provide accommodation for the elderly, the chronically sick, unmarried mothers, vagrants, and 'Part III' (healthy destitute) inmates. Many of the old workhouses were sold off, demolished, or fell into disuse. The day-to-day operation of the institution in Kirkby Stephen was managed by the North Westmorland Guardians Committee which, in 1938, dealt with 56 inmates under the direction of Mr William John Ion, Master.

Eden House PAI continued to serve the community of Kirkby Stephen until the post-WWII election of a Labour Government. Several relevant Acts were passed in 1945, 1946, and 1948 (1) and, notably, the 1948 (2) National Assistance Act. The latter formally abolished the last vestiges of the poor law system that had existed since the reign of Elizabeth I. As part of the creation of a unified public health-care system, free for everybody, rich and poor, at the point of delivery, many of the remaining workhouse buildings were converted into elderly residential homes, sold, or demolished.

Fig. 13 Drawing by Edward Frankland of the Workhouse in 1955.
Courtesy of Roger Frankland

Christian Head, a residential facility for the elderly in Kirkby Stephen
opened on 29th March 1961 with 41 residents. The old Workhouse
buildings (seen in **Fig. 13** while still in use in 1955) gradually
deteriorated to a state of significant disrepair. By the 1970s some of the
buildings had been used for a Sunday school, a shooting gallery, and as a
builder's yard, with some residential accommodation (owned by Peter
Davidson). He was the owner when it was sold for demolition. The old
Workhouse buildings were finally pulled down in 1974.

The story of Kirkby Stephen Workhouse had not quite concluded,
however. Historically it had been standard practice that, if an inmate died
in a Union Workhouse, and a relative could not be found who would
organise and pay for a funeral, then the Guardians would arrange a burial
in an unmarked grave in a local cemetery or burial ground. This would
have taken place in an area of a cemetery reserved for the purpose. In
Kirkby Stephen's case this area was situated to the north west of the
cemetery chapel. At the instigation of Reverend Roger Paul, the Vicar of

the Parish in 2002, and with the help of the Town Council and Margaret Birkbeck, Secretary of the Friends of Christian Head, sufficient funds were raised to erect a simple memorial stone on the site of the paupers' graves in the town's cemetery (**Fig. 14**). The stone was dedicated on 26th November of that year, a belated symbol of how the Workhouse cared for paupers both in life and in death.

Fig. 14 The inscription on the memorial stone reads: *In Loving Memory of the 632 Residents of Eden House Kirkby Stephen Workhouse Who Died Between 1837 and 1961 And Who Are Buried in This Cemetery, But Who Have No Other Memorial Known Unto God.*

Epilogue

Workhouses were not always the dismal, pitiless places they were often perceived or portrayed to be. Certainly there were occasional instances of awful cruelty and abuse (eagerly reported in the popular media of the time), but most indications are that the vast majority of workhouse staff showed understanding and compassion for the inmates and tried hard to act humanely despite the deterrent ideology underpinning the New Poor Law. The East Ward Union Workhouse is unlikely to have been an exception to this observation.

For many local people trapped by poverty, the East Ward Union Workhouse was a lifeline to their own and their family's survival, far preferable to the destitution and starvation outside its walls. After the initial hard-line approach of the New Poor Law, under one roof the Workhouse encapsulated much of the institutional care that is now provided for by the modern welfare state, namely:

- orphanages and schools for all children;

- maternity hospitals for children born in or out of wedlock;

- infirmaries for the treatment of accidents, infectious diseases, and more long-term illnesses;

- old folks' homes;

- residences for people with mental illnesses or learning difficulties;

- lodging houses for the homeless.

For more than 80 years the East Ward Union Workhouse in Kirkby Stephen provided the community's paupers and the needy with a vital safety net, and served its community well.

Appendix 1

For the purposes of this article, the main Acts of Parliament dealing with poor relief are these:

1552 Act for the Provision and Relief of the Poor;
1572 Vagabond Act;
1576 Act for Setting the Poor on Work;
1597 Act for the Relief of the Poor;
1601 Act for the Relief of the Poor, aka the Old Poor Law;
1662 Act for the better Relief of the Poor of this Kingdom, also known as the Settlement Act;
1723 Act Amending the Law Relating to Settlement, Imployment and Relief of the Poor. Knatchbull's Act, also known as the Work House Test Act;
1782 Act for the Better Relief and Imployment of the Poor, also known as Gilbert's Act;
1819 Select Vestry Act;
1834 Act for the Amendment and Better Administration of the Laws Relating to the Poor in England and Wales – the Poor Law Amendment Act (1834), also known as the New Poor Law
1945 Family Allowance Act;
1946 National Insurance Act;
1948 (1) National Health Service Act;
1948 (2) National Assistance Act.

Appendix 2: Report of the Commemoration Dinner Held at the King's Head Hotel April 1930

An edited version of the article that appeared in *The Herald* Saturday 5th April 1930.

A MERRY DEATH
East Ward Guardians Cheerful at their Passing
Appleby Solicitor Prepares their 'Last Will and Testament'

It is not usual for people to celebrate their own funerals, but this was what the East Westmorland Board of Guardians did at Appleby on Tuesday night, when the funeral rites of the Board were performed. The 'funeral tea' (though in reality it was a dinner), far from being a tearful affair, was a very jovial gathering, and the Board can at least be said to have died in good spirits.

The dinner was held at the King's Head Hotel [...] There was a large attendance of members of the Board from both the Kirkby Stephen and Appleby 'ends' and of officials. An excellent repast was served.

In proposing the toast of 'The late Board of Guardians', the Mayor said that he thought everyone would agree with him that the late Board was a body of men and women who had done their duty magnificently and sympathetically. He was very pleased to see them all looking so bright and cheerful that night because they were supposed to have passed away the night before, and this was to be their funeral. Happily, there had been no deaths or, at least, there did not appear to be any mourners, but if there were any he hoped they would accept his sympathy.

Mr C Harker [...] replying said it was something of a paradox that they should be toasting at the festive board, seeing that they passed into eternity the previous night. In Sir Walter Scott's *Quentin Durward* the Provost Marshall's hangman was said to be able to talk to his victims so persuasively that when he had finished they really believed that it was a better thing to die than to live, and went over to eternity rejoicing. That was exactly what had happened to them. The reason was that they were satisfied that in the past they had done their bit, and that it was not their fault that their job had been taken from them.

He went on that they [the Guardians] had all 'passed over' the night before, but some of them, in the twinkling of an eye, had risen again, and, as one of those, he regretted losing the association of so many old and trusted Guardians. They would carry on the work very much as they had done, but the associations would be entirely different. He was perfectly sure, however, that the poor would be well looked after because there was growing up a realisation of the fact that whether they were poor or rich, whether virtuous or degenerate, they were all members of the same family, and it was a desire as well as a duty to help the poor.

Mr P Udale [...] had not been able to find any precedent as to what a man said at his own funeral. They had, to put it bluntly, 'got the sack', and were met to commemorate the occasion. They had, however, been relieved of much exacting and unthankful work. He did not suppose many of them had accumulated much wealth by being on the Board [of Governors] but he thought they had managed to shuffle out conveniently without any medical assistance, and he thought they could say they had passed out honourably.

MR GUY HEELIS PREPARES THE WILL

Mr Heelis [...] said they had met to mark their regret at the passing of a body the like of which would not be seen again. It was not like the passing of an individual. In a man's lifetime he was referred to as a man, and on his death he became merely a body. In the lifetime of the Board it was a body, and now they had become merely men. They had died intestate. If they had made a will it would perhaps have been something like this: 'I, the East Ward Board of Guardians, being, as I firmly believe, of sound mind and understanding, but being nevertheless conscious of my approaching demise, do hereby declare this to be my last will and testament. I appoint the County Council of Westmorland to be my executors and trustees, and devise and bequeath to them all my institutional and non-institutional property and liabilities for their own use absolutely. I bequeath to the said County Council such of my officers and staff as they may in their absolute discretion consent to accept at my hands, such officials and staff to be free of death duties but to be liable to such other duties as they have hitherto performed. I give to my dear friend John Harker an annuity or yearly sum of such an amount as my executors may deem reasonable, such sum to be some compensation for him in his grief and sense of loss at my demise. Lastly, I leave to Neville Chamberlain, the Minister of Health, whom I blame for my present ill-health and my approaching end, my sincere wishes that his rabbits will die and the same to Sir Arthur Robinson with knobs on.'

The newspaper piece ends: ' [...] and as the company left the room the pianist humorously played the Dead March.'

Acknowledgements
Thanks go to Douglas Birkbeck, Wendy Coulthard, Joyce Davidson, Audrey Dent, Martin Holdgate, Lily Hornby, Margaret and John Gowling, Valerie Kendall, Ken Martin, Mark Peatfield, Jim Poulson, Ann Sandell, Raynor Shaw, Elizabeth and Peter Simms, Anne Taylor, Jean Thomson, Jenny Vincent, Ann and John Walton, Sheila Wilkinson, and Dave Williams. Special thanks go to Peter Higginbotham and R N Thompson.

SOURCES
Anderson, A. M. A. & Swailes, A. 1985. *Kirkby Stephen*, Kendal: Titus Wilson.

Birkbeck, D. 2000. *A History of Kirkby Stephen*, Soulby: Cito Press.

Braithwaite, J. W. 1884. *Guide to Kirkby Stephen, Appleby, Brough, Warcop, Ravonstonedale, Mallerstang, etc.*

Braithwaite, J. W. Undated. *Kirkby Stephen - where to go, what to see.*

Brundage, A. 1978. *The Making of the New Poor Law: The Politics of Inquiry, Enactment, and Implementation, 1832-1839.*

Brundage, A. 2001. *The English Poor Laws 1700-1930.*

Coulthard, W. Personal communication.

Crowther, A. C. 1981. The Workhouse System 1834–1929: The History of an English Social Institution, Batsford Academic and Educational.

Dent, A. Personal communication.

Emmison, F. G. 1966. *Archives and Local History.*

Extracts from the Court Roll of the Manor of Kirkby Stephen of Admissions to certain premises now the Factory up to the year 1747-1809.

Fowler, S. 2007. *Workhouse: The People: The Places: The Life Behind Closed Doors,* The National Archives.

Fraser, D. (Ed.) 1976. *The New Poor Law in the Nineteenth Century.*

Gibson, J. and Rogers, C. 2008. *Poor Law Union Records: 2. The Midlands and Northern England.*

Gowling, J. Personal communication.

Gowling, M. *Kirkby Stephen Charter Fair 1605.* Unpublished manuscript.

Higginbotham, P. 2006. *Workhouses of the North,* Tempus.

Higginbotham, P. 2012. *The Workhouse Encyclopedia,* The History Press.

Higgs, M. 2007. Life in the Victorian & Edwardian Workhouse, Tempus.

Journal of William Fletcher, Railway Missionary to the Workmen on the Settle & Carlisle Railway, 1870-1875. Transposed and compiled by Kay Gordon, with additional research by Margaret and Neville Pailing. Held at West Yorkshire Archives Bradford, Cat. No. 62D75/1.

Kelly's Directory 1906.

Kirkby Stephen Register 1773.

Kirkby Stephen Town Council Minutes, September 2000 and July 2002.

Longmate, N. 2003. *The Workhouse,* Pimlico.

Mannix & Whellan. 1847. *History, Gazetteer and Directory of Cumberland.*

May, T. 1987. *An Economic and Social History of Britain 1760–1970,* Longman Group.

May, T. 2011. *The Victorian Workhouse,* Shire Publications.

McKay, B. and Wilson, C. *Kirkby Stephen at Work 1780-1905 - a Historic Directory.*

Morris, Harrison & Co. 1861. *Commercial Directory & Gazetteer of the County of Cumberland.*

Morrison, K. 1999. *The Workhouse: A Study of Poor Law Buildings in England,* English Heritage.

Nicholson, J. & Burn, R. 1777 *The History and Antiquities of the Counties of Westmorland and Cumberland* Vols. I. and II. Reprinted 1976.

Parkinson's Guide and History of Kirkby Stephen And District. 1900. Reprinted 1926.

Parson, W. and White, W. 1829. *A History, Directory and Gazetteer of Cumberland & Westmorland.*

Peatfield, M. Personal communication.

Rose, M. E. 1971. *The English Poor Law 1780-1930 ,*Newton Abbot: David & Charles.

Rose, T. 1832 *Westmorland, Cumberland, Durham and Northumberland,* London.

Sharpe, J. A. 1987. *Early Modern England: a social history 1550-1760,* University of York, reprinted 1997, Bloomsbury.

Simms, E. Personal communication.

Slack, P. 1995. *The English Poor Law, 1531-1782,* Cambridge University Press.

Sowerby, R. R. 1950. *Historical Kirkby Stephen and north Westmorland,* Kendal: Titus Wilson.

Shepherd, M. E. 2004. *From Hellgill to Bridge End: Aspects of Economic and Social Change in the Upper Eden Valley 1840-1845,* University of Hertfordshire Press.

The Herald, Saturday April 5th, 1930.

Thomson, J. Personal communication.

Thompson, R. N. 1976. *The New Poor Law in Cumberland and Westmorland 1834-1871,* PhD thesis, Newcastle University, March. Carlisle library ref. 2A 362.5

Thompson, R. N. 1978. *The Working of the Poor Law Amendment Act in Cumbria, 1836-1871.* In Forster, G. C. F. (ed). 1979. *Northern History: A Review of the History of the North of England* Vol. XV, pp. 117-137.

Valuation Office Surveys 1910-1915, reference IR58.

Walton, J. & A. Personal communication.

Westmorland Gazette, 14th October 1845.

County Archives, Kendal:

- Board of Guardians minute books. Vol. 1 (1836) to Vol. 24 (1930). WSPUE;
- General ledgers. Vol. 7 (1864-1867), and Vol. 10 (1874-1879);
- Committee minute books 1862-1893. WSPUE/2;
- Assessment Committee minute books 1862-1873; 1909-1927. WSPUE 2/1;
- Register 1890-1957. WSPUE/4;
- Hothfield box 24;
- The Manufactory (later the Workhouse), Kirkby Stephen 1803-1818. WC/C/OL/743;
- various conveyances, admittances, and deeds. WC/C/OL 743/1 to WC/C/OL 743/14.
- Westmorland County Council Welfare Dept., register of births and deaths, Kirkby Stephen Workhouse 1874-1960. WC/W;
- Register of births and deaths at KS workhouse, 1874-1913. WC/W/1/41;
- Miscellaneous items 1794-1806. WC/W/1/27;
- Punishment books 1881-1905. WC/W/1/41 and WC/W/1/42;
- Deeds of former workhouse, KS 1840-1921. WDX385;
- Photo of Eden House. WDX 449/2;

- Kirkby Stephen parish list of workhouse inhabitants (notes made by Mr Goode). WDX 1222/2/8;
- Old papers 1636-1818. WDMG/5/1;
- Old papers 1771-1835. WDMG/5/2;
- Tithe awards no. 169 Kirkby Stephen, Hierarchy level 8 (Diocese of Carlisle); no. 2 plan of the township of KS in the parish of KS and county of Westmorland, by James Hay, Surveyor, 1839. WDRC/8;
- East Ward Union, John Clark, Master, 1st January 1869. WDY/276/2;
- Articles of Agreement 1818. WSMBK/5/24;
- Ordnance Survey maps: 1st edition 25" 1858; and 2nd edition 25" 1898.

FROM TRACKWAYS TO TRUNK ROADS: The Roles of Geology, Technology and Protest in Upper Eden
Raynor Shaw

Whether a settlement grows and prospers, stagnates or declines, is primarily due to its geographical location. Even with the benefits of modern technology, patterns of settlement and trade continue to be strongly influenced by local topography, soil types and other natural resources. The author has combined his geological knowledge with information from published sources to examine and explain the historical development of routes through and around Kirkby Stephen.

INTRODUCTION
Kirkby Stephen
Kirkby Stephen is a small market town in Cumbria's Upper Eden Valley, granted its first Market Charter in 1353. The town is situated on a north-south road (the modern A685) and set amid sparsely populated fells. Located at a fording- and later bridging-point of the River Eden, Kirkby Stephen became the focal point of a network of early routes, in particular from Sedbergh and the Lune Valley in the south, and along the Eden River through the Mallerstang valley. These roads continue to Brough, a nearby market town that is situated on the major Trans-Pennine route over the Stainmore Gap, to Appleby and to Penrith.

Significantly, the Upper Eden district lacks the important economic minerals that historically were mined in the Lake District to the west (*e.g.* Cameron & Mitchell, 2000), the Yorkshire Dales to the south (*e.g.* Morrison, 1998), the Mid-Pennines to the east (*e.g.* Raistrick, 1973), and Alston, Weardale and Teesdale to the north (*e.g.* Sopwith, 2015). Quarrying of limestone for building stones, lime-burning for agricultural lime, and more recently for water purification, has contributed towards the local economy. Agriculture has been the major occupation for thousands of years, the fertile, low-lying Vale of Eden being characterised by a relatively warm, dry climate and comparatively rich soils, particularly in the lower reaches of the valley. However, around Kirkby Stephen the floor of the Eden Valley is narrow, the soils are stony clays (glacial tills) that tend to be marshy, and the flat lowlands soon give way to steeper marginal land that is only suitable for hill farming and, latterly, grouse moors.

The County of Cumbria

Throughout history, the border region with Scotland that is now Cumbria has been fairly isolated within the United Kingdom, despite evidence of early human occupation dating back to around 12,670 – 9,600 BC.

The unusual northward alignment of the fertile Eden Valley provided a convenient route for Scottish raids, from late 13th century to the Union of the Crowns in 1603. Pele towers, castles and other defensive structures dot the Cumbrian landscape, testament to the turbulent past that characterised this disputed borderland over several centuries.

SETTLEMENTS AND GEOLOGY
The Location of Settlements

Many factors determine the location of settlements, the relative importance of these having changed over time. Determining factors can be grouped into two broad categories: the physical characteristics of the settlement site, and the location of the settlement within a hinterland (*i.e.* the ease, or otherwise, of communications), both factors being primarily controlled by the underlying geology.

Early populations were predominantly nomadic, hunting and gathering across the landscape. During the Neolithic Revolution (between about 8,000 - 10,000 years ago) there was a transition to a more settled existence that involved important developments such as the domestication of plants. Stationary populations required settlement sites that provided for their immediate needs, which included a reliable local water supply, ground free from flooding, a local wood supply for fuel and building, and a natural defensive position (*e.g.* high ground or within a river bend). Later developments in agriculture and industry led to the need for fertile soils, a favourable micro-climate, and the presence of raw materials such as coal, iron ore, limestone and building stone.

Geology and the Landscape

Local topography is controlled by the underlying geology, specifically the type of rocks and their history. Rocks are subjected to a variety of transformational processes, including jointing (fractures in rocks along which no movement has taken place), folding, faulting below the surface, and weathering when exposed to the atmosphere.

Fault systems play a major role in the evolution of the landscape. Faults are linear fractures in solid rock along which movement, vertical or horizontal, has taken place. Major faults, more correctly termed fault systems, are rarely discrete single fracture lines but usually consist of a relatively wide belt of fragmented and displaced rock. Relative displacements along faults can raise or lower adjacent blocks, thus directly creating uplands or lowlands, such as along the Pennine escarpment. Faults influence the scenery indirectly by creating zones of weakness (fractured and crushed rock) along which weathering (decay) and thus erosion (removal) of material is facilitated, as along the Dent Fault. Consequently, fault systems commonly determine the location, alignment and dimensions of valleys.

Details of the topography between fault zones depend on the composition of the underlying rocks, which determines their relative hardness *i.e.* resistance to weathering and erosion. Between major faults there are commonly areas of stronger, less-faulted, rock that form uplands. Superimposed upon these geological controls in Northern England are the effects of erosion and deposition during the Quaternary Ice Age, a period that profoundly influenced local topography and land use.

Since the last ice age, humans have become a conspicuous geological agent, transforming landscapes and erosion patterns through activities such as deforestation, agriculture, mining, urban development, and civil engineering works.

Geology and Topography in Upper Eden

The geological history of Britain, as interpreted from the surviving rocks, reveals a steady northward drift from southern latitudes to the present northern location. This migration was interrupted by episodes of continental collision and break-up. Distinctive rock types and diagnostic fossils, such as desert sandstones and equatorial forest trees, provide evidence of earlier latitudinal positions. Northern England exhibits a striking geodiversity that records these changes. The area is underlain by a wide variety of rocks with a geological history spanning almost 500 million years.

Down the centre of the region runs the broad, fertile lowland of the Vale of Eden, an important corridor that separates the main Lake District massif in the west from the Pennine escarpment in the east. The Vale of Eden is predominantly underlain by limestones and sandstones. Kirkby Stephen is situated on Carboniferous limestones of the Great Scar Group, which are overlain by glacial boulder clay. Sandstones include the distinctive Permian and Triassic (Permo-Triassic) age red desert sandstones, attractive rocks that have been quarried to construct many of the important buildings in the area, most notably Kirkby Stephen Parish Church. Permo-Triassic red sandstones continue eastwards to form spectacular cliffs at St Bees Head on the north-west Cumbrian coast and northwards beneath the Solway Firth lowlands. During early Permo-Triassic times the older Carboniferous limestones were uplifted to form a chain of mountains within a desert climate. Erosion of these uplands created large fans of angular limestone debris that was subsequently cemented by dissolved calcium carbonate to form a distinctive rock, a calcareous breccia. Known locally as Brockram, this rock was used to build many of the older houses of Kirkby Stephen.

The dome-shaped uplands of the Lake District define the western boundary of the region. Southwards and eastwards the ancient rocks of the Lake District massif descend below the Eden Valley, disappearing beneath a cover of younger Carboniferous rocks that crop-out around Kirkby Stephen. Pure Carboniferous limestone creates an area of distinctive karst scenery in the south, but in the west the Carboniferous sequence includes beds of coal, with haematite occurring in the limestone. These resources of coal and iron ore gave rise to the heavy industries of Workington, Whitehaven and Barrow-in-Furness.

High, desolate moorlands of the northern Pennines demarcate the east of the region. Rising gently westwards the moors attain an elevation of 893 m at Cross Fell, the highest point in the Pennines. The Pennine escarpment is underlain by sandstones and limestones of Carboniferous age. Towards the foot of the escarpment the Carboniferous rocks overlie Lower Palaeozoic rocks of Lake District character.

A distinctive feature of the north Pennine landscape is the terrace-like character of the hillsides. This morphology is created by the regular alternation of contrasting sedimentary beds within the Carboniferous succession. Relatively resistant sandstone or limestone beds form the steeper steps or scarps, and softer mudstones create the intervening terraces.

Towards the southwest, the rugged Pennine escarpment merges into the rounded, undulating hills and rocky crags of the Howgill Fells, an area that is underlain by Silurian slates and gritstones. Eastwards, the Pennine sandstones and limestones are replaced by the younger Carboniferous Coal Measures that underlie the Northumberland and Durham Coalfield, one of the earliest coalfields worked in Britain.

Quaternary glaciations were largely responsible for sculpting the upland landscapes of the region, while the intervening lowlands preserve a legacy of deposition in the form of drumlin fields. These elongate mounds of glacial debris swing westward across the southern and northern margins of the Lake District and extend eastward through the Stainmore Gap.

Major Fault Systems and the Northern Landscape

Major fault systems have determined the topography, and hence the pattern of valleys and trade routes, in and around Kirkby Stephen. The northern scenery, in particular the alignments of the valleys, can be interpreted from an examination of the major geological faults. These are depicted on the British Geological Survey 1:50,000-scale geological maps of the district (BGS, 1969; 1973; 1974a; 1974b; 1977; 1985; 1997a; 1997b; 1997c; 2004; 2007) and are summarised on the Map (**Fig. 1**).

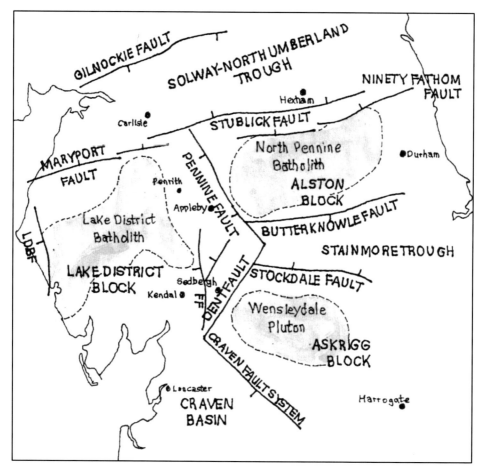

Fig. 1 The Major Fault Systems in Northern England
     LBDF = Lake District Boundary Fault. FF = Firbank Fault
     Note 1: Brough is located at the intersection of the PFS and DFS
     Note 2: The Stainmore Summit Fault strikes eastwards along the
          Stainmore Trough
     (Map drawn by Raynor Shaw: Compiled from several sources)

Faults characteristically form a rectilinear pattern, with individual fractures splaying, re-converging, and intersecting in a grid-like network. Major fault systems occur between rigid crustal blocks that are underlain by granite plutons (Appendix). These stable blocks are an important element of the regional geology of Northern England (**Fig. 1**). Within the blocks there is a comparative lack of folding and major faulting, any faults that do occur are generally shallower and less continuous.

The Pennine Fault System

The landscape of Northern England is dominated by the north-south spine of the Pennines, bleak moorlands that rise gently westwards to form the west-facing Pennine escarpment. This prominent feature was initiated during the Permian Period (299 to 252 million years ago) by vertical movements along the important northwest-southeast-trending Pennine Fault System (**Fig. 1**), a complex series of faults that have local names at several localities (**Fig. 2**). The western side of the fracture zone was down-faulted (dropped vertically) to form the broad Eden Valley, a major topographical feature that forms an important north-south corridor. Unusually for rivers in Britain, the River Eden flows northwards. Towards the west, the floor of the Vale of Eden rises gradually, reaching 977m at the summit of the Lake District massif.

Location	PENNINE FAULT SYSTEM Local Fault Names
North	Knock Pike Fault
	Murton Pike Fault
	Swindale Beck Fault
	Hilton Fault
	Thornthwaite Fault
	Roman Fell Fault
	Hillbeck Fault
	Augill Fault
South	Argill Fault

Fig. 2 Local fault names along the Pennine Fault System

The Pennine Fault System terminates in the north at the west-to-east-trending Stublick Fault System (**Fig. 1**), near Brampton, Carlisle. Significantly, the Stublick Fault System controls the alignment of the Tyne Valley, a strategic trans-Pennine corridor that is today followed by the A69 trunk road.

The Dent Fault System

In the south the Pennine Fault System terminates at the northeast-southwest-trending Dent Fault System, in the vicinity of Brough-under-Stainmore (**Fig. 1**). This fault system, in combination with the Rawthey Fault, dictates the alignment of the Rawthey Valley, an alignment that is followed today by the A683 Kirkby Stephen to Sedbergh Road. Just as the Pennine Fault System defines the western boundary of the Pennine Escarpment and the eastern edge of the Eden Valley, the Dent Fault System defines the western edge of the Askrigg Block, an ancient geological structure that underlies the Yorkshire Dales (**Fig. 1**).

Local Faults around Kirkby Stephen

Underlying the settlements of Brough and Winton is a complex structural pattern created at the intersection of the Pennine and Dent fault lines (Burgess & Holliday, 1979). The Augill Fault (**Fig. 1**) extends east-south-east from Brough crossing the Stainmore Summit as the Stainmore Summit Fault. This line determines the location of Stainmore Pass, an important trans-Pennine corridor that is followed today by the A66 Trunk Road. The Argill Fault extends southwards below the Kirkby Stephen district. Running almost directly west-east from near Kirkby Stephen is the Stockdale Fault that determines the location of the wide pass over Tailbrig and continues below the well-defined valley of Wensleydale.

The Craven Fault System

To the south, the Dent Fault System links to the Craven Fault System near Kirkby Lonsdale, an important fault that defines the southern boundary of the Askrigg Block (**Fig. 1**). The northwest-to-southeast-trending South Craven Fault System links with the Aire Valley Fault System. These two fault systems determine the alignment of the Aire Valley and the A65 trunk road that connects Kirkby Lonsdale with Settle and Skipton and eventually with Leeds.

Extending northwards from the intersection of the Dent Fault and the Craven Fault is the Firbank Fault. This structure controls the alignment of the Lune Gap south of Tebay, a feature that is followed today by the West Coast Main Line and M6 Motorway.

THE EVOLUTION OF TRADING ROUTES
Trade Corridors
Because few settlement sites can satisfy all the requirements of an expanding and evolving population, trading with other communities becomes necessary. Thus, depending upon the scale and regional distribution of agricultural or industrial production, routes are developed to transport crops, livestock and manufactured goods between population centres. The economic success of this shift from a subsistence to a market economy was dependent upon two primary factors, firstly the ease of communications and secondly the relative proximity and comparative wealth of the settlements in the region.

Early traders sought the shortest, least challenging routes, favouring those that were safe from attack and were well-supplied with food and water, both for the travellers and for their pack animals. Thus, in the rugged northern landscapes where the terrain is steep and often snow-covered in winter, routes generally developed along the valleys. However, while the valleys are typically more sheltered and less challenging than upland routes, particularly in winter, and provide more reliable water and grazing, the valley floors are commonly marshy. Consequently, tracks characteristically developed along the valley sides. This situation contrasts with the south of England where dry 'ridgeway' tracks, such as The Ridgeway and the Icknield Way along the crests of the rolling chalk downs, are more common (*e.g.* Ingrams, 1988; Rudd-Jones & Stewart, 2011).

From early times, networks of trade corridors gradually evolved across Britain; primary routes along which people, livestock and goods moved between two or more towns. Although topography is the primary factor that determines the pattern of routes, political constraints may influence the choice of routes at various times. Within any region, a hierarchy of trade corridors characteristically develops, dependent primarily upon the size and topography of the region, the relative strengths of the local economies, and the prevailing trading patterns.

Geology and Trade Routes
The underlying geology exerted a fundamental control upon the development of ancient trackways and medieval trade routes, and thus on the resulting settlement patterns, primarily through its influence on the topography and drainage patterns. Mountain passes, such as the Stainmore Gap, river valleys, such as the Eden and Rawthey valleys, and

fording and bridging points, such as Kirkby Stephen and Appleby, dictated the alignment of the early routes.

Rock type and geological structures determine the topography and the soil types, while at a particular latitude the topography modifies the local climate and vegetation associations. Geology directly influences population distribution and density in a variety of ways, primarily through determining the topography and the availability of natural resources.

Easily defended positions, such as natural fortresses, and flood-free settlement sites were early requirements. Available water resources are a function of the distribution and character of the local springs and rivers, and the effects of topography in promoting rainfall through orographic effects or by creating rain-shadows. Populations grew and prospered in areas with favourable topography and soils, which determined the availability and fertility of arable and grazing land. Local geology also dictated whether suitable building stones occurred locally. Water-borne and overland trading routes developed according to the dimensions of rivers and their valleys, and the character of mountain and river crossing points. Later in history the distribution of economic minerals dictated the location and development of mining and primary industries.

Significantly, the rocks of the adjacent northern Pennines are traversed by veins of valuable metal ore. Mining has underpinned the economy of the area since Roman times, despite severe changes in fortune over the period. During the 19th century mining boom, lead, silver and zinc ores were the primary targets, succeeded in the 20th century by baryte, fluorspar and witherite. Locally, barytes and fluorspar were mined around Brough. Although mining has now largely ceased, the legacy of this once important industry is still discernible in the pattern of routes and settlements that cross the region from the east.

Civil Engineering and Social Attitudes
During the Industrial Revolution in Great Britain (around 1760 to 1840), advances in civil engineering practice overcame successively greater topographical constraints to route alignments through the development of embanking, bridging and tunnelling techniques. Civil engineering improvements led to a greater appreciation of the role of geology in facilitating or hindering construction projects. Indeed, the first geological map of England (1815) was compiled by William Smith, the 'Father of Geology', from discoveries that he made while surveying the routes for

canals in southern England (Winchester, 2002). Despite modern technological improvements, geological conditions are still a vital factor in the location of new transport routes. Adverse geological conditions encountered while surveying a preferred alignment can result in a route being relocated to a cheaper (and more safely) engineered, although not necessarily the most direct, alignment.

Changing political conditions and social attitudes also influence decisions about infrastructure projects. Factors such as local enterprise, bold regional or national leadership, and technological advances have steered the development of trade patterns, countering many of the inherent geographical limitations, and influencing the location of new settlements. Also, in more recent times, government statutes, planning regulations, national quotas, and taxation regimes have imposed administrative constraints upon the type and volume of goods produced, and hence transported and traded, by particular economic activities. Crucially, public protests have become more common and increasingly influential over the last century.

However, no amount of private initiatives, government intervention, or public pressure can fundamentally alter the intrinsic properties of the regional or local geology and landscape.

The Development of Trading Routes in Upper Eden
Particular trade routes originated, were consolidated, and later superseded, primarily in response to the evolution of land transport modes, but also to advances in civil engineering practice. Thus, the early trade routes to and from Kirkby Stephen can be directly linked to the features of the local topography, *i.e.* the pattern of faults, a fundamental determinant that was progressively supplanted by technological advances. The development of these routes is considered in relation to the evolution of land transport, and the concomitant advances in civil engineering and changes in public attitudes.

Footpaths and Tracks
Early humans necessarily travelled on foot, typically following game. Routes would probably have crossed low passes and followed the sides of river valleys, the floors being marshy or heavily wooded. Archaeological investigations have uncovered the remains of many early dwellings and settled communities, but direct evidence of connecting trackways is harder to find. However, there is indisputable evidence that pre-historic

inhabitants travelled, or at least traded, extensively around the British Isles. For example, in Northern Britain, between about 2,730 BC and 2,550 BC, fine-grained volcanic tuffs (lithified volcanic ash) were sourced from screes at an elevation of about 1,800 feet above sea level, on the flanks of Pike of Stickle in Great Langdale in Cumbria. These were roughed-out *in situ* before being transported to several lowland sites for polishing and hafting. Finished stone axes were then widely traded, with examples being found as far afield as the Isle of Man, south-west Scotland, the Lothians, Yorkshire, and southern England (Rollinson, 1996, pp.15-16; Hindle, 1977, pp.6-7; Fell, 1950). Clearly, important commodities were being traded along well-established trading routes, and between communities over 300 km apart, at least 4,500 years ago.

In the Upper Eden district there is evidence of important settled locations, such as late Neolithic to early Bronze Age (around 3,500 – 1,000 BC) stone circles (*e.g.* Long Meg and Glassonby) and Croglam Castle, an Iron Age (800 BC – 100 AD) defensive settlement at Kirkby Stephen.

An intriguing structure near Kirkby Stephen is the Nine Standards, a row of nine dry-stone cairns. These are located on the Pennine watershed at the highest point of the local skyline (650m above sea level), about 5 km from the town centre. Although their age and origin are still the subject of speculation, archival research has confirmed that they existed at least 500 years ago, and possibly more than 3,000 years ago (Walker, 2008). Their dominating position suggests that the cairns have probably, from early times, served as waypoints and landmarks for travellers along the Eden Valley and across the Pennines. Indeed, 'Viewshed' analyses (Friends of the Nine Standards, 2014) have demonstrated that the features are visible from a very wide area on both sides of the Pennines. Recent remote-sensing investigations have revealed indications of buried structures around the site, further supporting the view that the location was probably an important meeting point for Neolithic hunters, Bronze Age herders, nomadic pastoralists and possibly long-distance traders.

Even at this early stage political factors possibly played an important role in determining the choice of trading routes. Until the Roman invasion of Britain, regional tribal groups such as the Carvetii (present-day Cumbria), Brigantes (Northern Pennines) and Votadini (Northumbria) controlled large sections of the country. Their influence upon the passage of traders through their territories is difficult to determine, although they certainly presented a challenge to the Roman occupiers.

Early Roads

Although the wheel was invented about 3,500 BC, in the region that is now Iraq, the concept of road building arrived much later. Expansion of the Roman Empire, from about 312 BC onwards, was accompanied by the construction of road networks across their territories to facilitate the rapid movement of troops.

Following their invasion of Britain in 43 AD, the Romans progressively asserted their control by building, generally straight, military roads across the country, as well as introducing milestones (Benford, 2002). Around 69 AD they defeated the Brigantes, a powerful local people who controlled the territory of Briganteum, and Roman legions were sent north to secure the region.

Many Roman roads followed the fault-valleys, for example along the Stainmore Pass, the Eden Valley and at the foot of the Pennine escarpment through modern-day Brough, Kirkby Thore, Brougham and Penrith. Much of this route is now under the modern A66 Trunk Road. Forts along the route included *Lavatris* at Bowes, Maiden Castle 8 km to the east of Castle Brough, and *Verterae* Fort at Castle Brough. Excavations at *Verterae* Fort yielded large numbers of lead seals from amphora (wine jars), coins, ornaments, and brooches (Ecroyd-Smith, 1866). Roper Castle (also known as Round Table) is a Roman signal station, high on the moor on the western flank of Moudy Mea, about 10 km east of Brough and 1.6 km south of the Roman road. East of the Pennines this road would have connected to Dere Street, which ran between *Cataractonium* (Catterick) fort and *Eboracum* (York), the latter a fortress and capital of the Roman Province of Britannia.

Less certain, but speculated upon by several authors (*e.g.* Margary, 1973 - Road Number 731; Anderson & Swailes, 1985, pp.10-11; http://www.romanroads.org/gazetteer/cumbria/M731.htm) is a Roman road along the Dent Fault System, from Sedbergh up the Rawthey Valley to Kirkby Stephen, which joined the Stainmore Road at Church Brough. Although the old road utilises the valley followed by the modern A683 it is, for the most part, higher up the valley side (**Fig. 3**).

Fig. 3 Roman Road along the Dent Fault System. (Photograph by Raynor Shaw)

The existence of an old trackway is not in doubt, but the Roman origins are more circumstantial, relying largely on place names such as Bluecaster Side, Borwens and Street. Thus, from south to north, are Street Road (across Fell End), Streetside farm, the hamlet of Street, The Street and Street Farm. In addition, the route is considered to be a direct-alignment and well-engineered, with a classic Roman dog-leg descent and ascent to cross the River Rawthey to the east of the present Rawthey Bridge. The lack of proved connections at the northern and southern ends lead some to doubt the authenticity of the attribution.

Interestingly, the deep and straight Mallerstang valley is not fault-controlled, but was gouged-out of the limestone beds by ice. There may have been a Roman road along the side of the valley from Church Brough, via Nateby, Water Yat and Hell Gill to Wensleydale. Tantalising evidence occurs in the form of a discovery, in 1926, of a hoard of Roman coins, from 'Sleddle Mouth' on Mallerstang Edge. 'Sleddle Mouth' is interpreted today as 'Steddale Mouth' (Grid Ref. NY 802 007) (Mattingley & Collingwood, 1927). Another interpretation of what is, in places, a well-engineered road, is that Lady Anne Clifford, Countess of Pembroke, Dorset and Montgomery (1590-1676) was responsible for directing improvements to an older trackway to facilitate her journey between family estates at Skipton Castle and Pendragon Castle. Indeed, the route high up the valley side is known locally as 'Lady Anne's Highway'.

Droving

From Romano-British times (43 to 410 AD) onwards, drovers moved large numbers of livestock around the country. Many drovers' routes followed similar alignments to the earlier Roman roads. Other routes coincide with manorial or parish boundaries, suggesting that they probably had pre-Roman origins as ancient trackways. Drove roads are characteristically wider, between 40 feet (12 metres) and 90 feet (27 metres) than the Roman military roads (8 ft [2.45 m] wide where straight, and 16 ft [4.90 m] wide where curved), to accommodate large herds of cattle or flocks of sheep. They also had wide verges for stock to graze. The droving tradition persisted into the early 19th century, declining initially in response to agricultural improvements, and terminating with the advent of the railways in the 1840s. Many drove roads were subsequently metalled and incorporated within the UK highway network.

Cattle droving has a long and well-documented history in Cumbria, particularly in the Eden Valley. From the 17th century to the 19th century, thousands of cattle were driven southwards from Scotland down a network of droving routes taking them to new pastures in the Yorkshire Dales and then onwards to market. Ancient trackways through the Eden Valley were used by the Abbots of Bolton Abbey (1120 – 1539) and Fountains Abbey (1132 – 1539) who moved their animals in a seasonal cycle. This practice, termed transhumance, involved driving their flocks from winter grazing in the Borrowdale valley to home pastures in the spring. However, it is generally held that cattle were more important to the Cumbrian economy than sheep, particularly because they survived the journeys better. Notably, the 9th Earl of Thanet reared cattle cheaply in his lands in the Upper Eden Valley prior to them being driven south to his main property at Hothfield in Kent where they were pastured and restored in preparation for being profitably sold in the London market (Roebuck 2015, pp. 82-83).

The droving ways from Scotland chiefly converged on Carlisle, continuing south towards Penrith. From there an extensive network of drove roads spread out across Westmorland and North Yorkshire (Bonser, 1970). One major western valley route ran via Shap, Orton and Tebay to Kirkby Lonsdale. Another route followed the Eden Valley to Brough, with one branch continuing over Stainmore and another to Kirkby Stephen. An upland route to the east ran via Tan Hill to Reeth in Wensleydale, then continued to Richmond.

Another important droving route, which is generally considered to follow a medieval trading way, ran south from Kirkby Stephen through the Mallerstang Valley. Nicholls (1883, p. 64) recorded the names of the former inns in Mallerstang that were used by drovers, in particular the tale of Betsy Ward (*Rapsy Bett*) who kept the Black Bull. 'Scotchmen' (*sic*) who drove their cattle and sheep through Mallerstang to the Craven district of Yorkshire would put up at her house for the night. Beyond Aisgill, the route branched eastwards along 'The Highway' towards Hawes and Wensleydale, or continued to the Moorcock Inn from where it turned eastwards towards Hawes or westwards towards Dent. From here the route went on to Thornton-in-Lonsdale, or via Garsdale and Dentdale to Gearstones (Ribblesdale), from where the drovers followed several routes south to markets in Lancashire.

Research indicates that in 1697/1698 a total of 59,701 Scots cattle crossed the Scottish border (Roebuck, 2016, p. 51), which had increased to 100,000 by 1800 (Haldane, 2015). This traffic had the effect of transforming the Cumbrian economy from a simple subsistence existence to a buoyant market economy, banking and commerce thriving on the success of the droving industry. Inns to accommodate and revitalise the drovers prospered, and there were greens or enclosures for overnight pasturing. Important fairs and markets grew up at towns such as Brough, Kirkby Stephen and Hawes, where stock was sold and replacements purchased. Impoverished farms became profitable and related tradesmen, such as tanners, saddlers, girdlers, cordwainers, and cobblers all prospered. The hides were used for leather, fat for candles and soap, hooves for glue, and hair to strengthen plaster. Local carriers also benefitted by transporting the manufactured goods.

Packhorses and Carriers

Following the collapse of the Roman Empire, the road network in Britain deteriorated into dirt tracks that became muddy and almost impassable in winter. During the Middle Ages (5th to 15th centuries), although some merchants travelled the rutted roads in horse-drawn covered wagons, the most common mode of transport was on horseback. Stout packhorses (or 'sumpter horses') with large panniers slung over their backs proliferated, travelling in long columns of up to 50 horses. Packhorses continued to be used until the construction of the first turnpike roads (from the 1630s onwards).

From monastic times onwards, long trains of laden packhorses would have been a common sight on the northern hills, particularly in the mineral-rich North Pennines. Packhorses carried a wide range of goods, including wool, cloth, hides, coal, iron ore, lead, charcoal and salt, often over considerable distances, and particularly between Yorkshire and Lancashire (Raistrick, 1978). The favoured horses were sturdy Galloways and 'Jaggers' (German 'Jaegar' horses). As a consequence, the droving route south from Kirkby Stephen to Gearstones (Ribblesdale) was known as 'Galway Gate', and the drovers were colloquially known as Jaggers.

Many packhorse routes survive today, typically because they crossed higher ground and were less likely to be obliterated by later turnpikes or surfaced roads, and also because many were paved with flags where they crossed wetter areas. Some packhorse routes are distinguished by the presence of packhorse bridges, which are characteristically narrow, allowing only single-file passage, and feature low parapets that would not interfere with the large panniers. Although packhorse routes and bridges are well-documented in the Lake District region of Cumbria (*e.g.* Bray, 2009), they are less well-recorded in Upper Eden. However, several packhorse bridges have been preserved in and around Kirkby Stephen. These include Frank's Bridge in Kirkby Stephen (**Fig. 4**), Church Bridge over Dalebanks Beck in Crosby Ravensworth, Smardale Bridge over the Scandal Beck, the bridge over Rais Beck near Orton, the bridge over Chapel Beck in Orton, and Ben's Bridge over the Clough River in Garsdale.

Fig. 4 Frank's Bridge in Kirkby Stephen. (Photograph by Raynor Shaw)

Tan Hill Inn occupies the site of a stage house on an important Pennine route used by packhorse trains carrying coal from local coal fields, as well as cattle drovers travelling down from Scotland. Nicholls (1883, p.61) records the memories of one Mr Geo. Blades, who described the packhorses coming down Mallerstang from Cotterdale and Swaledale, and heading to Kirkby Stephen. Mr Blades particularly recalled 'noticing their wooden saddles, on which they tied bags, *etc.*'.

The legacy of the drovers and packhorses is preserved in the names of certain localities and public houses. For example, the word *hollins*, a Scottish dialect word, refers to the hollybushes that the drovers planted on the hill-top routes to mark the way. Today, Hollin near Sedbergh, Hollin Hall near Crook, and Hollins View at Brough Sowerby are survivors from that era. Fording points are reflected in the place name *wath* or *wathe* today (*e.g.* Wath near Newbiggin-on-Lune). Public houses bearing names such as 'The Scotsman', 'The Packhorse', and 'The Black Bull' hark back to that era.

Turnpikes
During Tudor times (between 1485 and 1603) roads were rutted dirt tracks, despite the fact that parishes were legally obliged to maintain the roads in their district. Roads improved markedly after 1663 when the first Turnpike roads were opened. Improvements continued during the 18th century with the formation of 'Turnpike Trusts', Acts of Parliament that gave wealthy patrons the responsibility of improving and maintaining specified roads, and the right to charge travellers a toll. Between 1751 and 1772, a period known as 'Turnpike Mania', 389 new turnpikes were enacted. Although most were to improve existing roads rather than build new routes, the turnpike system established about 32,000 km (*circa* 22,000 miles) of improved roads.

Although the first Turnpike Trust was established by an Act of Parliament in 1663, Cumbria did not participate in the turnpike movement until 1739, by which date 100 Turnpike Trusts had been established around Britain. By 1838 there were 169,000 km (105,000 miles) of public highways in Britain, of which 35,000 km (22,000 miles) were turnpikes (Wright, 2008, p.21).

Within the Upper Eden area, the Bowes-Brough road was turnpiked in 1743, and the Brough-Eamont Bridge road in 1753 (Gowling, 2011, p. 118). Subsequently, the Appleby-Kendal road, the Orton-Shap road, and the Tebay-Brough road were turnpiked in 1761. From 1761 the Sedbergh Turnpike Trust began to construct several turnpikes radiating from Sedbergh, including the Sedbergh-Kendal road and the Sedbergh-Grayrigg road, which were turnpiked in 1762. The Kirkby Stephen-Sedbergh-Greta Bridge road was completed in 1765, following the alignment of the modern A683 via Rawthey Bridge. The Sedbergh Turnpike Trust erected stone milestones along the length of all their roads in 1814. These were later replaced by cast iron mileposts beside the Kirkby Stephen route. Several of these survive today.

In 1769 there was an application to extend the Bowes-Brough turnpike southwards from Maiden Castle through Kaber to Brough and Kirkby Stephen. Other proposed routes included turnpikes from the Stainmore Turnpike to Taylor Rigg, and to transport coal from Tan Hill to King's Pitts in Yorkshire, as well as a route from Tan Hill to Reeth (Gowling,

2011). Much later, in 1825, the road between Kirkby Stephen to Hawes was turnpiked. Leaving Kirkby Stephen, the road followed the Mallerstang valley to the Moorcock Inn at Garsdale Head where it joined the existing Sedbergh-Askrigg turnpike. Milestones placed along this route are of a similar design to those adopted by the Sedbergh Trust.

A distinctive, and in many cases surviving, feature of the turnpikes are the tollhouses that were built beside the tollgates at each end of the turnpike to collect the tolls from passing travellers. Around the country the appearance, and in some cases flamboyance, of the tollhouses reflect both the regional building styles and the economic prosperity of the region (Wright, 2008). Some of the known tollhouses around Kirkby Stephen are listed in **Fig. 5** and illustrated in **Fig. 6**.

GATE NAME	MAP REF.	PARISH	LOCATION	STREET NAME
Molds, Coal Rd	NY 87719	Stainmore	Kaber Fell (Barn)	Molds Hill (Old Barn)
Low Gill	NY 77644 15260	Brough	The Gatehouse	Low Gill Cottages, Flitholme, South of Bale Hill
Milking Stile	NY 80505	Brough	Milkingstile Cottage	Middleton Road
Bollam Lane	NY 77567	Kirkby Stephen	Bollamgate Cottage	Nateby Road
Rigg	NY 78286	Kirkby Stephen	Gate House	Mallerstang, Outhgill, Ing Hill
Kirkby Stephen	NY 773 080---	Kirkby Stephen	N of Market Square	Demolished
Coupland Beck	NY 71165	Warcop	Toll Bar Cottage	Coupland Beck (SE of CB Farm)
Borrowbridge	NY 605 015	Tebay	Long Borrow Bridge	Demolished?
PrimarySource: http://www.turnpikes.org.uk/Tollhouses%20of%20Westmoreland.htm				

Fig. 5 Tollhouses in the Kirkby Stephen area

Fig. 6 Milkingstile Cottage, Middleton Rd, Brough. (Photograph by Raynor Shaw)

Stagecoaches and The Royal Mail
Introduction of the turnpikes enabled wheeled conveyances to become more widespread. Around 1600, the royal posts were the exclusive preserve of the king, but in 1635 Charles I granted royal approval for members of the public to pay his messengers to carry their letters. Thus, the Royal Mail was born (Mountfield, 2003). Initially used only for letters (mail coaches), fare-paying passengers were later allowed. By the middle of the 17th century stagecoaches, so called because they worked in 'stages' between coaching inns, provided regular timetabled services between the major towns.

Cumbria, in common with most regions of Britain, did not have roads suitable for wheeled vehicles until the late 18th century. Indeed, Cumbria was reputed to have some of the poorest roads in the country, 'a most confused mixture of rocks and bogs' (Williams, 1975). This situation prevailed, in spite of the fact that the economy was expanding and the population increasing, particularly in the towns. The advent of the turnpikes improved some roads, making them suitable for coach travel.

However, stagecoach travel was expensive, the un-sprung coaches were uncomfortable on what were still rutted roads, and passengers were in danger of attacks by highwaymen. Indeed, Nicholls (1883, p.62) recorded that, prior to the introduction of the railways, the road through Mallerstang was '*sequestered and dangerous for travellers to venture owing to highwaymen, three especially who lived in the dale. Their names were Ned Ward, a native of the dale, who lived at Farclose House; Riddle, who was a border man; and Brodrick, who seems to have come from Orton. These men seem to have been highwaymen of the magnanimous stamp that is to say, they would not rob the poor or any of their neighbours; indeed, though their practices were known, they were in a certain sense respected by their neighbours.*'

The most important coach to pass through Kirkby Stephen was The Lord Exmouth, which ran from Lancaster to Newcastle-upon-Tyne via Barnard Castle. This service departed from the King's Arms in Lancaster at 0400 hours, and arrived in Newcastle-upon-Tyne at 1900 hours, travelling at an average speed of about 11 mph. Fares were £3 17s 6d for an inside seat and £1 18s 9d, half price, to sit on top. The journeys consisted of eight stages, each of about 14 miles, between inns and horse changes. These stages were: Lancaster – Toll House at Clafton/Hornby – Kirkby Lonsdale – Sedbergh – Kirkby Stephen – Barnard Castle – Bishop Auckland – Durham – Newcastle-upon-Tyne (Clowes, 2018, personal communication). In 1829 The Lord Exmouth departed from the King's Arms in Kirkby Stephen for Newcastle-upon-Tyne at 1000 hours, and Lancaster at 1500 hours, a journey of about 6 hours (Birkbeck, 2000, p. 59).

However, it is quite possible that the route was operated as two distinct contracts, at least in 1836. Thus, according to Bates (1969, p.109), the 1836 licence for the 60-mile service from Lancaster to Barnard Castle was held by J. Dunn and Co., who offered one return journey daily. The company had two coaches (Licence Nos. 9581 and 9586) that could each carry 4 inside and 5 outside passengers. The 40-mile service from Newcastle-upon-Tyne to Barnard Castle is shown as being operated by J. Radford & Co., who offered one return journey on Tuesday to Saturday, and one single journey on Sunday and Monday (Bates, 1969, p.124). This company had one coach (Licence No. 9829) that could carry 4 inside and 9 outside passengers.

There is little information about any other long-distance coach services passing through Kirkby Stephen, although in 1829 there were 'carriers' operating weekly services from Kirkby Stephen to Brough, Appleby, Ravenstonedale, Orton, Mallerstang, Hawes, Sedbergh, Kirkby Lonsdale and Lancaster (Parson & White, 1829), some of which carried passengers, albeit in rather austere conditions amid the freight. Carriers also offered three services a week to Kendal, and weekly services to more distant destinations, such as Manchester, Preston, Chorley, and Newcastle-upon-Tyne (Birkbeck, 2000, p.61). Scheduled stagecoaches departed daily from Liverpool, travelling to numerous destinations across the north of England and passing through Kendal, Shap and Penrith on route to Carlisle, Durham and Newcastle (Arkle, 1921).

Coaching inns were a particular feature of coaching routes. Kirkby Stephen had several inns including the existing King's Arms and Black Bull, and now demolished Sun Inn that was located on the north-eastern corner of Market Square (Birkbeck, 2000, p.59). What is now the Cross Keys Temperance Inn on the Cautley road was, in the early 1800s, High Haygarth farmhouse. Conversion to a coaching inn is believed to have occurred shortly after 1819 when the Cautley road (A683) was re-aligned. Originally higher up the slope on Bluecaster Fell, the line of the suspected Roman Road, the new road occupied a lower-level route that passed in front of High Haygarth. Brough had nine coaching inns in 1829, the main stop being the White Swan on the busy Penrith to Stainmore Trans-Pennine route.

The Canal Era
The first transport revolution began in 1759 when the Bridgewater canal opened. During the period of 'Canal Mania' between 1760 and 1840, about 3,200 km (*circa* 2,000 miles) of canals were built in Britain, supplementing 3,400 km of navigable rivers. Canals replaced packhorses, transforming trade in areas that were favourable for canal building. Railways rapidly followed the canals after 1840.

Kirkby Stephen was never in contention to attract a canal, given that it was not a manufacturing centre for high-value, heavy items, nor a mining area. In addition, the topography of the district was ill-suited to canal building. The nearest canal connected Kendal with Lancaster, opened in 1819 (Satchell, 2001). Even below Carlisle the River Eden is not navigable, so the river trade never developed in the Eden Valley. However, the River Eden and its vigorous tributaries did power several mills in and around Kirkby Stephen. These included corn mills, a fulling mill, and a sawmill. There were also mills in surrounding villages such as Brough and Hartley.

The Railway Era

The second transport revolution began with the opening of the Stockton and Darlington railway in 1825, closely followed in 1830 by the Liverpool to Manchester railway. These lines heralded the period of 'Railway Mania', during which railway building connected most towns in Britain. Interestingly, the arrival of the railways heralded the demise of the highwayman. Britain's railway network reached its greatest extent in 1914 when there were 37,720 route km (23,440 miles) of track.

Significantly, the railways benefitted from the revolutionary developments in civil engineering that were pioneered by the canals. Firstly, whereas the early roads were subject to the constraints imposed by the topography, following valley floors, adhering to contours, or traversing passes, canals introduced the techniques of cutting, tunnelling, embanking, and aqueduct (viaducts for railways) construction that enabled them to follow more direct alignments between destinations (**Fig. 7**). Although detailed route-surveys were carried out to determine favourable alignments, never before had the natural obstacles presented by the topography been so directly challenged and successfully overcome.

Fig. 7 Smardale Gill Viaduct. (Photograph by Raynor Shaw)

Secondly, the railway companies benefitted from the skills learned and perfected by the navvies (or 'navigators'), the teams of migrant labourers who built the canals. Indeed, the experienced navvies moved almost seamlessly into building the new railways (Coleman, 2015). By the 1850s the railways presented a threat to the canal operators whose cargoes had fallen by over 60%. Many struggling canal companies were bought out by railway companies, either to remove competition, or to build a railway along the line of the canal. Locally, the owners of the Lancaster Canal, 'The Company of Proprietors of the Lancaster Canal Navigation', initially leased the northern end of the canal at Kendal to the London and North Western Railway (LNWR) on the 29th July 1864, finally selling the section to the LNWR on the 1st July 1885.

Railway construction in Upper Eden began with the Stainmore Line, a trans-Pennine route connecting Barnard Castle in the east to the West Coast main line at Tebay. The directors of the Stockton & Darlington Railway were interested in a railway to Westmorland that would extend westwards their existing line from Darlington to Barnard Castle, which was opened on the 8th July 1856 (Walton, 2013, p.11). Their main consideration was the need to carry Durham coke to the iron works at Barrow-in-Furness, and haematite (iron) ore to Cleveland, a case of the bounties of regional geology indirectly benefitting Kirkby Stephen. The decision to route the main line from Barnard Castle to Tebay, and not Penrith, was ascribed to the influence of one Mr Joseph Pearce, a director of the Stockton & Darlington Railway. Fellow directors concurred that the shortest, and most economical route, to Furness was south to Tebay to join the Lancaster & Carlisle line. This proposal created a controversy that was ultimately resolved by forming two railway companies, the South Durham & Lancashire Union Railway and the Eden Valley Railway (Walton, 2013, p.11).

The South Durham & Lancashire Union Railway appointed Thomas Bouch as Chief Engineer, with the responsibility to overcome the many engineering challenges along the rugged route. These included the construction of several large viaducts, notably the 200-foot high Belah cast-iron viaduct and the 550-foot long Smardale Gill stone viaduct (**Fig. 7**) to span the deep valleys along the alignment. Ceremonial cutting of the first sod took place at Kirkby Stephen on the 25th August 1857 (Walton, 2013, p.75), and the opening celebrations were held on the 7th August 1861.

Sir Richard Tufton of Appleby Castle aided by local grandees supported the second line, the Eden Valley railway, linking the South Durham & Lancashire Union Railway at Kirkby Stephen with the West Coast main line at Clifton, near Penrith. The first sod was cut at Appleby in 1858, and the line was opened in 1862 (Birkbeck, 2000, p.68).

The third line, a much more challenging engineering undertaking, was the Settle-Carlisle line, a 72-mile-long south-to-north route built by The Midland Railway Company. Major structures comprise 325 bridges, 21 viaducts (including the iconic Ribblehead Viaduct with 24 arches) and 14 tunnels (Anderson & Fox, 2014). Indeed, so demanding was the terrain, the route climbing to 335 metres above sea level at its highest point, that the Midland Railway placed two of the original twenty stations, those at Dent and Kirkby Stephen, above and outside the two settlements. Construction of this last great mainline railway in Britain began with the cutting of the first sod at Settle in 1869. The line officially opened for goods traffic in August 1875, and for passengers on the 1st May 1876.

Kirkby Stephen was profoundly influenced by the arrival of the railways, both during the periods of construction and subsequent operation of the three lines, transforming it into a railway town for 100 years. The population, which stood at 1,141 persons in 1801, had increased by 24% to 1,664 by the 1881 census, a rise attributable to the number of jobs created in the town by the three railways.

Increasing competition from road transport, beginning in the 1920s and accelerating in the 1930s, posed severe challenges to both passenger and freight services on the railways. Declining passenger numbers resulted in the last passenger train running from Tebay to Kirkby Stephen on the 1st December 1952. The line was kept open for freight and mineral traffic to Hartley Quarry (opened in 1926) until January 1962 when both the Stainmore and Eden Valley lines ceased through-freight operations. The track from the dedicated sidings at Hartley limestone quarry to Appleby remained open until the 31st October 1975: another benefit of favourable local geology. Following this final closure the line was lifted. What is striking is that the 1952 and 1962 closures predated the two reports by Dr Richard Beeching ('The Reshaping of British Railways' of 1963, and 'The Development of the Major Railway Trunk Routes' of 1965, both published by the then British Railways Board) that are generally held to be responsible for the termination of numerous rail services. Thus, although national public protests against the 'Beeching Cuts' did result in the saving of some stations and lines around Britain, Kirkby Stephen had lost passenger services at its East Station a decade before these cuts were announced.

Although the Settle-Carlisle line had survived the earlier rounds of closures, by the 1980s plans were being made to discontinue this line, with British Rail claiming that the line was costing millions to maintain. Express trains from London and the Midlands to Scotland and freight traffic were withdrawn, and eight of the smaller stations, including Kirkby Stephen West, were closed. Then, in keeping with the growing protest movements of the times, public pressure to keep the line open mounted. The Friends of The Settle-Carlisle Line and the Joint Action Committee were formed, with a campaign launched on the 15th December 1983. One notable early success of the publicity campaign was to increase passenger journeys on the line from 150,000 to 450,000 a year. After a six-year struggle, the Government announced on the 11th April 1989 that it had rejected the British Rail plan to close the line. Today, a little over a quarter of a century later, about 1.2 million passengers travel on this scenic railway each year.

Thus, what began as an audacious project to conquer some of the most inhospitable terrain in Britain, where 'the Victorian engineers were playing God with his own creations' (SCRDC, 2010), was mirrored, a little over a century later, by overwhelming public pressure that overturned the decisions of a major nationalised body.

Motorised Road Transport
Concomitant with the development of steam-powered railways was motive power for road vehicles. Although Nicolas-Joseph Cugnot demonstrated a steam road locomotive in Paris in 1769, steam wagons were not common until the mid-1800s. Significantly, the adoption of these early machines was held back by the powerful 'horse lobby' (Kidner, 1975), an early example of the powerful influence of special interest groups. The first lorry powered by an internal combustion engine appeared in 1895, petrol-engines being used until the first diesel-powered lorry was introduced in 1923. Motor coaches first appeared in the early twentieth century and private cars, although launched in 1885, were not universally affordable until after World War II. By 2018 there were 31.6 million private cars on UK roads and 5 million commercial vehicles moving 1.9 billion tonnes of goods around the country.

The increase of motorised vehicles required fundamental changes in how the road system in the United Kingdom was funded and operated. The Ministry of Transport, founded in 1919, devised a road classification system to designate the major routes across the country. The 'Roads Act 1920' introduced a 'Road Fund' that enabled Government to receive revenue for road building and maintenance through an excise duty on road vehicles. County Councils were responsible for all roads in 1930, but in 1936 the Ministry of Transport published the Trunk Roads Act, which gave Government direct control of the core road network.

During the heyday of coach travel Kirkby Stephen was a regular stopping-off point for holiday coaches from the northeast to the coastal resorts of Lancashire. From 1928 to around 1983, Primrose Coaches operated a daily service between Tyneside and the Fylde Coast, with one coach in each direction. Scheduled stops were made in Kirkby Stephen. However, in recent years faster vehicles have reduced the journey time, and the installation of on-board toilets and drink machines have precluded the need for a mid-route tea and rest stop. Although coaches still pass through the town, technology has replaced the once vital function of the cafés and public toilets of Kirkby Stephen.

Kirkby Stephen has experienced some of the vicissitudes of 20th century changes in road transport and public opinion. For example, the A685 road that runs southwards from Brough to Kendal, via Kirkby Stephen and Tebay has seen changing fortunes. Following the lifting of the track on the former South Durham & Lancashire Union Railway, the formerly winding country road between Newbiggin-on-Lune to Tebay, through Kelleth and Gaisgill, was realigned along the old track bed. The road was subsequently 'trunked', a trunk road being a major road between important destinations that is the recommended route for long-distance and freight traffic. In 1974 the Kirkby Stephen Parish Council approached the County Council to build a by-pass around the town (Birkbeck, 2000, p.64). However, the County Council finally abandoned the idea of constructing a Kirkby Stephen bypass in 1997 (CWH, 2000), in part due to the protestations of local traders who feared losing business. Concerns were, in part, due to the experience of nearby Brough that was physically separated into Market Brough and Church Brough by the construction of the A66 bypass in 1977. The new road diverted through traffic from the main street past the town with an attendant loss of business.

Public pressure following the Kirkby Stephen decision resulted, in October 1999, in a temporary ban being imposed upon heavy goods vehicles using the A685 between the A66 at Brough and the M6 at Tebay. The road haulage industry lobbied to have the restriction lifted when the trial period ended in May 2001. Concerned residents along the A685 protested, in the interests of more peaceful lives with a lower risk of accidents. Consequently, the ban was made permanent, and the road was de-trunked. Road hauliers are now legally required to travel via Penrith, almost twice the distance, and diverting 400 more heavy vehicles a day through other small towns such as Temple Sowerby and Kirkby Thore. Increased pollution because of the extra miles travelled, extra running costs of £1.9 million for the freight industry, and 64,000 more working hours a year have been cited (CWH, 2000). In this case, public opinion overrode the intrinsic geographical advantages of the more direct A685 alignment.

More recently, the Yorkshire Dales National Park was officially extended from the 1st August 2016, adding 417 square kms to the park, and bringing the boundary close to Kirkby Stephen. Consequently, the town has taken on a new role as 'The Gateway to the Dales' given the proximity of the town to the popular natural attractions of the Lake District and the Yorkshire Dales. Although the full effects of this administrative change are yet to be realised the decision will, it is hoped, maintain, if not revitalise, trade and travel along the routes through Kirkby Stephen.

SUMMARY AND CONCLUSIONS
What is clear from this brief review is that the alignments of the original routes through Upper Eden were dictated by the topography, which is a reflection of the underlying geology. Thus, ancient routes followed valleys and passes, with minimal engineering intervention.

Over time, technological advances brought about improvements in both civil engineering methods and transport modes. These gradual developments underwent a profound acceleration during the Industrial Revolution, which marked a major turning point in history. New processes and machines, in particular the invention of the steam engine, allowed the designing and excavating of canals, the building of railways, and audacious civil engineering works that together wrought major industrial, economic, social and cultural changes. The increasing ability of humans to engineer their environment is a hallmark of the period since the Industrial Revolution. Indeed, the impacts of humans on the Earth's geology and atmosphere have become so profound over recent centuries that geologists are now debating the designation of a new geological epoch termed the 'Anthropocene' (*e.g.* Lewis & Maslin, 2015) that will recognise the increasing power of humanity to affect the Earth's processes and systems.

Societal controls also underwent significant changes over this period, witnessing a transition from the powers of feudal landlords, wealthy Barons and autocratic monarchs, to the laws and interventions of elected Governments. More recently public protest movements have increasingly influenced local and national Government initiatives. Thus, although public protests are not a modern phenomenon (*e.g.* Stevenson & Quinault, 1974), modern media has enabled comment and dissent to be more rapidly and more widely disseminated (*e.g.* Roberts, 2014). Public protests are particularly vociferous over Government infrastructure plans, particularly with regard to transport routes such as bypasses, motorways and high-speed rail lines, and have proved themselves capable of influencing Government decisions. Particular examples in Upper Eden include the rejection of a Kirkby Stephen town-bypass, the de-trunking of the A685 road, and the saving of the Settle-Carlisle Railway.

In conclusion, it can be confidently stated that whereas the earliest route-finders and -builders had to negotiate their way around the obstacles presented by the natural landscape, modern route-builders have now to deftly chart a course that avoids or complies with the additional hurdles presented by complex legislation, Government bureaucracy, and the force of public opinion.

ACKNOWLEDGEMENTS
The author would like to thank Arthur Littlefair for informative discussions and instructive site visits during the early stages of this study. Thanks are also due to many people have sown the seeds of some of the ideas developed in this article, both during casual conversations and at Upper Eden History Society lectures. Their stimulus is appreciated.

APPENDIX : Granite Plutons and Stable Blocks

Granite plutons are large, mostly concealed, bodies of igneous rock that have congealed from molten magma deep below the surface. Plutons are rigid bodies that have roots extending into the mantle. They exhibit considerable variations in shape and size. Their importance is that they underlie what are termed crustal blocks, relatively stable areas that owe their rigidity to the presence of these massive granite bodies.

Concealed plutons are detected by gravity surveys. Regional variations in the strength of the gravity field, termed gravity anomalies, reflect the relative density of the rocks below the surface. Negative gravity anomalies, which are characteristic of masses of rock that are less dense than average, are typically associated with granite plutons. Once located, plutons are classified by their overall shape and size, and by their relationship to the surrounding rocks. Batholiths are the largest of the pluton types, vertical- or near-vertical-sided bodies that have a plan-area of at least 100 km^2. Smaller granite bodies of indeterminate shape or size retain the generic descriptor 'pluton'. Three plutons have been identified under massifs in the north of England (**Fig. 1**).

The Lake District Batholith underlies the Lake District Block in the west, cropping-out at the surface in places as the Eskdale and Shap granites. Gravity surveys indicate that the subsurface areal extent of the Lake District Batholith is more than 1,500 km^2, with an abrupt western margin that is coincident with the Lake District Boundary Fault (**Fig. 1**). This granitic batholith was emplaced during a period of intense volcanic activity between about 460 – 449 m.y. ago.

Underlying the Alston Block to the east is the Weardale Granite of the North Pennine Batholith, emplaced during the Early Devonian about 400 m.y. ago. This concealed body, which is about 60 km by 25 km in areal extent (*circa* 1,500 km^2), was first detected by gravity surveys. Drilling of the Rookhope borehole in the early 1960s encountered the granite at a depth of 390 m. Subsequent gravity surveys and drilling of the Eastgate borehole in 2004, which encountered granite at a depth of 270 m, defined the form of this pluton.

Lying to the south is the Wensleydale Pluton, which underlies the Askrigg Block. Initially detected by regional gravity surveys, drilling of the Raydale Borehole in the 1970s confirmed the existence of the Wensleydale Granite at 495 m below the surface. The Askrigg Block formed a structural-high (upland) during the early Carboniferous (*circa* 359 – 323 m.y. ago) upon which the distinctive limestones of the Yorkshire Dales were deposited.

REFERENCES

Anderson, A.M.A., & Swailes, A. (1985): *Kirkby Stephen*. Anne M.A. Anderson & Alec Swailes, Kirkby Stephen.

Anderson, V.R. & Fox, G.K. (2014). *Stations & Structures of the Settle & Carlisle Railway: Including Track Layouts, Signalling Diagrams & Illustrations*. Second Edition. Oxford Publishing Company/Ian Allan Publishing, Hersham.

Arkle, A.H. (1921). Early Liverpool Coaching. *Transactions of the Historic Society of Lancashire and Cheshire*, Vol. 73, pp 1-32.

Bates, A. (1969): *Directory of Stagecoach Services, 1836*. David & Charles, Newton Abbot.

Birkbeck, D. (2000): *A History of Kirkby Stephen*. Cito Press, Kirkby Stephen.

BGS (1969). *England and Wales: Sheet 32 Barnard Castle: Bedrock Geology*. 1:50,000 Scale Geology Series, British Geological Survey/Natural Environment Research Council.

BGS (1973). *England and Wales: Sheet 25 Alston: Solid and Drift Geology*. 1:50,000 Scale Geology Series, British Geological Survey/Natural Environment Research Council.

BGS (1974a). *England and Wales: Sheet 24 Penrith: Bedrock Geology*. 1:50,000 Scale Geology Series, British Geological Survey/Natural Environment Research Council.

BGS (1974b). *England and Wales: Sheet 31 Brough-under-Stainmore: Bedrock Geology*. 1:50,000 Scale Geology Series, British Geological Survey/Natural Environment Research Council.

BGS (1977). *England and Wales: Sheet 26 Wolsingham: Bedrock Geology*. 1:50,000 Scale Geology Series, British Geological Survey/Natural Environment Research Council.

BGS (1985). *England and Wales: Sheet 51 Masham: Bedrock Geology.* 1:50,000 Scale Geology Series, British Geological Survey/Natural Environment Research Council.

BGS (1997a). *England and Wales: Sheet 40 Kirkby Stephen: Solid and Drift Geology.* 1:50,000 Scale Geology Series, British Geological Survey/Natural Environment Research Council.

BGS (1997b). *England and Wales: Sheet 41 Richmond: Solid and Drift Geology.* 1:50,000 Scale Geology Series, British Geological Survey/Natural Environment Research Council.

BGS (1997c). *England and Wales: Sheet 50 Hawes: Solid and Drift Geology.* 1:50,000 Scale Geology Series, British Geological Survey/Natural Environment Research Council.

BGS (2004). *England and Wales: Sheet 30 Appleby: Bedrock Geology.* 1:50,000 Scale Geology Series, British Geological Survey/Natural Environment Research Council.

BGS (2007). *England and Wales: Sheet 39 Kendal: Bedrock Geology.* 1:50,000 Scale Geology Series, British Geological Survey/Natural Environment Research Council.

Bonser, K.J. (1970). *The Drovers: Who They Were and How They Went; An Epic of the English Countryside.* MacMillan, London.

Bray, R. (2009). *Walking on Bridges: Walks Along the Packhorse Routes and Bridges of the Lake District.* Hayloft Publishing, Ltd., Kirkby Stephen.

Burgess, I.C. & Holliday, D.W. (1979). *Geology of the Country Around Brough-under-Stainmore: Memoir for 1:50,000 geological sheet 31 and parts of sheets 25 and 30.* Institute of Geological Sciences, Natural Environment Research Council, London, Her Majesty's Stationery Office.

Cameron, A.D. & Mitchell, M. (2000). *Lakeland's Mining Heritage: The Last 500 Years.* Cumbria Amenity Trust Mining History Society, London.

Coleman, T. (2015). *The Railway Navvies: A History of the Men Who Made the Railways.* Head of Zeus Ltd., London.

Mattingley, H. & Collingwood, R.G. (1927). The Mallerstang Hoard. *Transactions of The Cumberland and Westmorland Antiquarian and Archaeological Society*, Vol. 27, pp 205-217.

CWH (2000). Public Inquiry Over A685 Lorry Ban?. *Cumberland and Westmorland Herald*, 16th September 2000.

Ecroyd Smith, H. (1866). Some interesting features of a neglected Roman station, Brough-under-Stainmoor'. *Transactions of the Historic Society of Lancashire and Cheshire*, New Series, 6, pp 137–52.

Fell, C. (1950). The Great Langdale Stone-axe Factory. *Transactions of The Cumberland and Westmorland Antiquarian and Archaeological Society*, New Series, Vol. 50, pp1-14.

Friends of the Nine Standards (2014). http://www.ninestandards.eu/final%20report.html

Gowling, M.E. (2011): *The Story of Brough-under-Stainmore*. Hayloft Publishing, Ltd., Stainmore.

Haldane, A.R.B. (2015). *The Drove Roads of Scotland*. New Edition, Birlinn Limited, Edinburgh.

Hindle, B.P. (1977): *Lakeland Roads: From Early Tracks to Modern Highways*. The Dalesman Publishing Company Ltd, Clapham.

Ingrams, R. (1988). *The Ridgeway: Europe's Oldest Road*. Phaidon Press, London.

Kidner, R.W. (1975). *Military Traction Engines and Lorries 1858-1918*. The Oakwood Press, Blandford.

Lewis, S.L. & Maslin, M.A. (2015). Defining the Anthropocene. *Nature,* 519, pp 171–180.

Margary, I. D. (1973). *Roman Roads in Britain*. John Baker, London.

Mountfield, D. (2003): *Stage and Mail Coaches*. Shire Album No. 416, Shire Publications, Ltd., Princes Risborough.

Morrison, J. (1998). *Lead Mining in the Yorkshire Dales*. Dalesman Publishing Co., Ltd., Skipton.

Nicholls, Rev. W. (1883). *The History and Traditions of Mallerstang Forest and Pendragon Castle*. John Heywood, Manchester.

Parson, W. & White, W. (1829). *History, Directory, and Gazeteer, of the Counties of Cumberland and Westmorland*. Edward Baines & Son, Leeds.

Raistrick, A. (1973). *Lead Mining in the Mid-Pennines*. Bradford Barton, Truro.

Raistrick, A. (1978). *Green Tracks in the Mid-Pennines*. Moorland Publishing Company, Nottingham.

Roberts, J.M. (2014). *New Media and Public Activism: Neoliberalism, the State and Radical Protest in the Public Sphere*. Policy Press, Bristol.

Roebuck, P. (2016). *Cattle Droving Through Cumbria 1600-1900*. Bookcase, Carlisle.

Rollinson, W. (1996). *A History of Cumberland & Westmorland*. (The Darwen County History Series) Second Edition, Phillimore & Co. Ltd., Chichester.

Rudd-Jones, N. & Stewart, D. (2011). *Pathways: Journeys along Britain's Historic Byways, from Pilgrimage Routes to Smuggler's Trails*. Guardian Books, London.

Satchell, J. (2001). *Kendal's Canal: History, Industry and People*. Kendal Civic Society, Kendal.

SCRDC (2010). *The Settle Carlisle Railway: A Guide to Your Journey Leeds-Settle-Carlisle*. The Settle Carlisle Railway Development Company, Limited, Settle.

Sopwith, T. (2015). *An Account of the Mining District of Alston Moor, Weardale and Teesdale*. Aziloth Books, Rookhope.

Stevenson, J. & Quinault, R. (Editors) (1974). *Popular Protest and Public Order: Six Studies in British History, 1790-1920.* Allen and Unwin, London.

Walker, S. (2008). *Nine Standards: Ancient Cairns or Modern Folly?.* Hayloft Publishing, Ltd., Kirkby Stephen.

Walton, P. (2013). *The Stainmore & Eden Valley Railways: A Pictorial History of the Barnard Castle to Tebay and Penrith Lines.* Oxford Publishing Company/Ian Allan Publishing, Hersham.

Williams, L.A. (1975). *Road Transport in Cumbria in the Nineteenth Century.* Allen and Unwin, London.

Winchester, S. (2002). *The Map That Changed the World: A Tale of Rocks, Ruin and Redemption.* Penguin Books, London.

Wright, G.N. (2008). *Turnpike Roads.* Shire Album No. 283, Shire Publications, Ltd., Oxford.

PART 3: PLAGUE

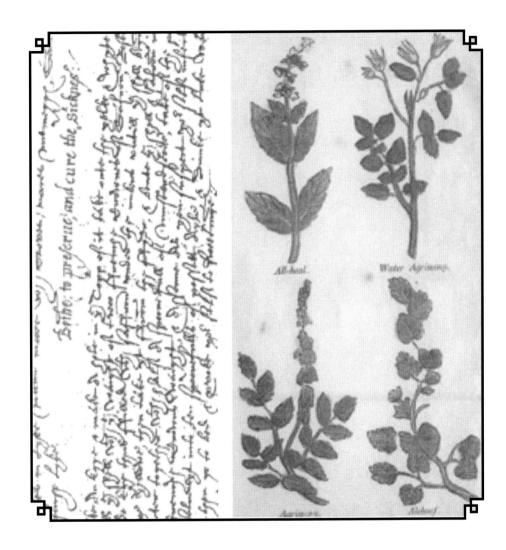

Left: 'Both to preserve and cure the sickness' copied with permission from Cumbria Archive Centre, Carlisle, from a 16th century manuscript D/MH/10/7 Vol I, p81. Right: some medicinal plants from Culpeper's 'Complete Herbal'.

KIRKBY STEPHEN AND THE PLAGUE
David Albert Mann

*The recent discovery of a 'plague stone' in the garden of a house just outside Kirkby Stephen (**Fig. 1** below) was the starting point for this in-depth study of the plague, particularly the late 16th century outbreak which had such a devasting effect in the north of England. The author has used a range of sources to chart the spread of the disease as well as discussing the actions and reactions of the clergy in a period when religious beliefs and emerging scientific thought were beginning to clash.*

Fig. 1 Plague Stone, just outside Kirkby Stephen

Various diseases and epidemics in historical times were grouped under the general denomination of the 'plague'[1]; the Black Death ravaged most of Britain and much of Continental Europe in the fourteenth and fifteenth centuries. In 1554 in Penrith and Kendal (and various other parts of England) there were outbreaks of something similar which caused the characteristic pustules and blisters on the skin. The infection which then followed in 1587-88 seems to have been typhoid, because of its different seasonal pattern (Mullet p.102);[2] but in the meantime in London the conventional plague was active every summer throughout much of the later sixteenth century, and especially so in 1592-93 when there were 11,503 deaths. In 1597-98 a pandemic, which is the subject of this paper, swept across northern England and resulted in terrible mortality in Cumberland and Westmorland. It returned again in 1623, and further south there was huge loss of life in the 1630s and again in 1665-66, after which it seemed to die out as Britain entered the 'Little Ice Age'.

Characteristics of the Plague

The traditional view held until recently was that this was the Bubonic Plague brought from the east, a coccobacillus (*Yersinia pestis*) which primarily infested rats, and once it had killed all the rats in a particular vicinity was passed to humans by the rat flea (*Xenopsylla cheopis*). This could then, it was thought, take the form of a pneumonic plague, a type of bubonic plague which was highly infectious and was transmitted without an intermediary through droplet infection i.e. sneezing, coughing etc.

In 1996 this view was challenged by a team of scientists from Liverpool University.[3] They argued that only the brown rat (*Ratus norvegicus*) had the capacity for this task, but that did not arrive in Britain until the eighteenth century, a century and more after the 1597-98 pandemic; its native cousin the black rat (*Rattus rattus*) being too restricted in its range and habitat. Instead they suggested the possibilities of anthrax at least as a contributory factor, especially since Penrith was a centre for the tanning trade and, as a consequence, anthrax was known locally as the *Cumberland disease.* (Mullett p.108)

It is a highly infectious disease characterized most commonly by local skin lesions or malignant pustules, and can be spread easily from person to person; it is a disease of domestic animals including, in order of susceptibility, goats, sheep, cattle, horses, pigs and dogs, which become infected by ingestion or inhalation of spores. The spores develop when the bacillus comes into contact with oxygen, and they form rapidly at high temperatures; temperatures of 20°C or less slow down spore formation. Anthrax spores are long-lasting, can live outside an infected body for long periods of time, and remain viable in the soil for at least 15 years. The spores are easily carried in the air or on skins, furs or wool, and for this reason anthrax is also known as the wool-sorter's disease. It is an occupational hazard for farmers, butchers and tanners, with imported goat hair, goatskin and carpet wool being the source of most human infections today. Although human infection is almost invariably from animal sources it can spread from man to man, and the incubation period is normally only 1 to 3 days. Pulmonary anthrax is one form of the disease where bacilli are inhaled from infected hair or wool, and death occurs within 1 to 4 days of the onset. (Scott & Duncan 1996 pp.18-19)

Although they warn that 'there is only circumstantial evidence to support this hypothesis,' they go on to point out the frequency with which earlier plagues were associated with increased mortality in cattle. When the

130

Scots drove 4,000 English cattle north in 1380, it was not all that they took, for they carried the plague with them as well.

Spread either by travellers carrying spores in wool packs or by drovers with infected animals implies that market towns would be particularly susceptible to anthrax, and it is noteworthy that it is in these rural centres that the plague epidemic became established in the Eden Valley. (Ibid p.19)

In subsequent publications Scott & Duncan have shifted their position in respect of the 'infectious agent' and, whilst rats and their fleas continue to be dismissed, anthrax has been replaced by an unidentified 'emergent disease' and put into the same category as Ebola and Aids (and, alas, stock-piled the world over).[4]

These infections are called haemorrhagic, and their characteristics include many of the same features formerly associated with the Bubonic plague, such as:

carbuncles, blains and the buboes, which were swollen lymph glands in the neck, armpit and groin [...]. Along with the swellings, victims experienced fever and high temperature, continual vomiting, diarrhoea and prolonged bleeding from the nose [...] accompanied by madness and delirium [...]. The causative agents of these diseases are called 'filoviruses'. They have a high fertility rate and tend to occur in explosive epidemics driven by person-to-person transmission. Outbreaks occur unpredictably; there is no treatment and, as yet, their animal reservoir is unknown [...]. (Scott & Duncan 2004 pp.222-225)

On Table 3, p.5, Scott & Duncan 1996 list all the occupational details of the householders taken by the plague in Penrith. It is interesting to note, in the context of the possible association of anthrax and *a propos* of spores being carried in skin, furs or wool, that by far the largest numbers in occupational categories targeted by the disease are those working in crafts to do with these materials – 8 shoe makers and cordwainers (leather workers) & 10 of their families, 5 glovers with 6 families, and 5 tailors also with 6 families. Along with smiths, these four crafts attract as many fatalities as the remaining 21 crafts put together.

Although Scott & Duncan are, in their later work, inclined to question the traditional view that plague was brought to Eyam in 1665 by a box of old

131

clothes, it is important to recognize the significance of second-hand clothing to an Elizabethan economy built since the Middle Ages on the creation and export of fabric. There were very few ready-made garments and apart from the very rich, almost everyone in an urban community would have worn second-hand clothing with, if they were lucky, linen under it made from flax, grown and processed on the farm. Elizabethan outfits were made in many parts; the sleeves for example were separate from the bodice or doublet, tied together with laces or 'points' and the elaborate decoration applied afterwards and removable. It was all very expensive and cherished and each item passed down this food-chain separately until it became rags used in the new paper mills or stuffed into the building's cavities as insulation, the metal lace melted down and used again.[5] It would have remained a prime source of infection.

Interestingly the disease affected only two out of the fifteen or so tanners then working in Penrith and three of their families, but popular superstition had it that tanners themselves were immune – 'a tanner will last you nine year,' says the Gravedigger in *Hamlet*, 'his hide is so tanned with his trade that it will keep out water a great while' (V.ii.168-72), along with shoemakers (though not so here) and smokers. (Barnes p.171) In fact there is now considerable evidence to suggest that immunities did develop (hence, it is thought, a lower incidence amongst the old).

In their most recent book Scott & Duncan (2004 pp.208-09) argue that those resistant to plagues, perhaps as many as 14% of the population in some areas, inherited a genetic mutation in the *CCR5* receptors of their white blood cells; this is called *CCR5-Δ32*. It is the same genetic mutation that presently protects bearers from the infections of HIV and AIDS and first manifested itself in the Black Death in the fourteenth century:

Although this mutation occurs at a high frequency in Eurasian ethnic-populations today, it is absent among native sub-Saharan African, American Indian and East Asian ethnic groups. This might explain the rapid spread of HIV in sub-Saharan Africa, whereas possession of the mutation may have delayed its progress in Europe.

Thus, whilst it is likely that most of those in the towns in Cumbria in 1597-98 would have come into contact with the disease (and 63 families became extinct), three-quarters of households in Penrith experienced only one or two deaths, whilst of the 316 families, 74 remained completely unaffected. (Scott & Duncan, 1996, p.4)

Plague and Famine
The 1597-98 visitation had originally been sea-born, spreading from Newcastle (where it had been recurrent since 1570), and down the Great North Road, infecting Durham and Darlington on the way. It passed over Stainmore and then seems to have struck out widely in our area at much the same time. The presumed carrier, one Andrew Hogson, 'a strainger', was buried in Penrith on 22 September, but before the first native victim, Elizabeth Railton (whom it is presumed he must have infected) could be buried on 14 October, the first burials were already reported at Kendal and Carlisle, both on the third of that month.

Richmond had already been infected in the August, and Dumfries was to follow. In Penrith plague arrived in September, flourished through until Christmas, was almost dormant during January and February, and then re-emerged with a vengeance in the New Year, rising to a peak in the summer months, dwindling again with the onset of winter in November and December, but not finally coming to a rest until 6 January 1598.[6] The closely packed, often insanitary, streets and ginnels of the towns were its primary breeding ground, but even some villages were affected.

With the increased interest in local history in the late nineteenth century, parish registers were scoured for evidence of plague in the country parishes; in many cases only the letter 'P' separated plague and non-plague deaths. Could it be that in some cases the higher than normal incidence of mortality might be a better guide to the presence of plague than a single, perhaps easily forgotten, letter? In the surviving records of 1597-98 there is much to go on, but also a problem for this line of reasoning.

At the end of the sixteenth century Britain was experiencing markedly lower mean winter and summer temperatures than usual. During the 1590s poor weather led to poor harvests for four successive years up to 1597. 'Remember the Spring was very unkind by means of the abundance of rains; our July hath been like a February, our June even as an April, so that the air must needs be corrupted,' said a preacher at York (Barnes p.179). Food prices rose first 30%, and then 36%, 83% and 65% and scarcity accompanied this inflation. The less well-off could not afford to eat properly, and this made people weak and more prone to illness.[7]

'Many have come 60 miles from Carlisle to Durham to buy bread' the Dean of Durham wrote to Lord Burghley on 10 January 1597 (Barnes p.178). Thus starving people left their land to seek succour in the towns. At Ravenstonedale on 6 January 1602 'Lewis Procter [was] starved in the snow'.[8] The details of the individual deaths in the Greystoke parish records for 1623 are unusual, and striking in their compassion:[9]

March 27th   *A poor hunger starved beggar child*
March 21st   *John Clementson of Jonby a poor man destitute of means*
               to live
September 11th*Leonard, son of Anthony Cowlman of Johnby late*
               deceased, which child died of want of food

These descriptive phrases, 'destitute of means to live' and 'died of want of food' recur over and over again. It was a calamitous time; the poor and starving died in barns, in people's houses, during church services, in a hogg-pen, even at the Town Cross where 'the yonge child of a poore begger of the pishe of Broughton' expired. 'Over a period of less than two years,' says Howson, 'nearly twenty deaths from starvation are recorded and in many more cases starvation is implied by the nature of the entry'.[10]

The adjective 'poor' today almost universally signals compassion, but in previous ages it tended to have a more technical meaning. The Elizabethan State had tried to see vagrancy as a crime wilfully committed rather than a consequence of failing agriculture, and in 1572 had sought to discourage the movement of indigents over fourteen years of age from one parish to another.

At which Session or Goale Delyverye yf such person or persones bee
duelye convict of his or her Rogishe or Vacabondes Trade of Lyef [...]
that then ymmedyatlye he or shee shalbe adjudged to bee grevouslye
whipped and burnte through the gristle of the right Eare with a hot Yron
of the compasse of an Ynche about [...].[11]

They were then to be returned to their own parishes, with death as the punishment for a third conviction, but the parish burial registers indicate that with the numbers on the move it could not be controlled in this manner. *The Act for the Relief of the Poor*, 1601, moving slowly from punishing paupers to their 'correction', envisaged an elaborate scheme to be administered by the parish. The 'impotent poor' – lame, old and blind -

were to be cared for in an almhouse or poor-house. The 'able-bodied poor' were to be set to work in a House of Industry; materials to be provided; and the 'idle poor' and vagrants were to be sent to the House of Correction; whilst pauper children would become apprentices. Outdoor relief, however, continued to be the main form of relief during this period because of the cost of the buildings in setting all this up. It was to be paid for by a poor rate levied on each owner or tenant in the parish; hence relief came not, as today, out of some magical centrally administered porridge pot, but directly out of the pockets of other members of the parish, and in a subsistence economy, ever on the margin, in most cases little better off themselves.

According to Scott & Duncan (1996 p.4), something in the region of 170 recent arrivals to Penrith, many of them 'vagrants in search of food and not native to the parish', perished in the plague. All the more remarkable then that only 9 victims of the plague are designated as 'poor' in the parish records. Many of the others would be selling what little they had for food, and perhaps too they paid for their funeral expenses. In Carlisle, the city medical officer Edward Alburgh provided all the medicine and plasters for the sick and attended the poor without a fee, and was presumably paid by the city to do so.[12] Thus it was that many parishes in the region registered higher-than-normal deaths in 1597 and in the years immediately preceding it.

Gosforth, which averaged 13 burials a year, had 56 deaths in 1596 and 116 in 1597; Greystoke with an average of under 30, had 182 in 1597; according to J.D.F. Shrewsbury, there were 'excessive mortalities' in 1597-8 in the parishes of Crossthwaite, Penrith, Newton Regny, Kendal, Kirkby Lonsdale, Crosby Garret, Cartmel, Heversham, and Middleton,[13] (but none of these have registered plague deaths). With these and so many more in the frame as possible plague sites, it seems apposite to list all the locations in Cumbria for which there is current evidence. Of the three largest towns, Penrith, Kendal and Carlisle, I shall deal *inter alia*; but, for completeness, extracts from the parish records of the smaller communities will be found in the Appendix: Appleby (128 deaths); Blatarne in the parish of Warcop (8 deaths); Brough-under-Stainmore (17 deaths); Edenhall (46 deaths); and Shap (3 deaths).

Kirkby Stephen and the Plague
Why then are there no records of the plague in Kirkby, the only centre of population of any size in the area not known to have been so blighted? By

the end of the sixteenth century it was a thriving little town, probably bigger than Appleby, at twelve miles distant, and certainly considerably bigger than Brough, only four miles away, both of which suffered from the plague.[14] It had its own weekly market with a royal charter, drawing traders from outside the area, and, as now, was on a major east-west route. It most probably had facilities of some sort for entertaining travellers, the prime source of infection. In 1538 Thomas Cromwell, then Henry VIII's Vicar General, required all parishes to record births, marriages and deaths, and despite, according to Howson (p.29), their unpopularity many parishes have faithfully done so ever since. Records for Penrith and Brough are fairly complete for the 1597-98 period, as are those of Edenhall, Warcop and Shap. Kendal's are incomplete but supplemented by corporation records.[15] Carlisle's parish records do not survive for this period but it has a list of households 'visited' i.e. affected by the plague and verified, but only up to 20 December 1597 (Hughes p.53). Appleby is dependent on a series of entries in an eighteenth century compilation of records,[16] and only Kirkby Stephen has no records at all for this period that might have shown the plague – if it had visited then – for its surviving parish records do not begin until 1667, half a century and more after the plague had struck the surrounding area. It has to be asked therefore whether it is this accident of history that has served to give the town the special status of being supposedly free of such disease?

At least one significant location has no official records of plague for this epidemic, but it does have traditional associations, which gives it a kind of status in this discussion:

In Keswick there is a tradition that when the plague raged, as no markets were held for fear of the infection, the people of the dales carried their webs and yarns to a large stone, which is very conspicuous on one of the lower elevations of Armboth Fell, and there periodically met and did business with the trades. The stone still goes by the name of the 'web stone'. Mr J. Fisher Crosthwaite informs me he has heard old people say that when the plague was in Keswick the country people came to 'Cuddy Beck', but did not cross the little stream. The money was placed in the water and then taken, and the produce was laid on the ground for the Keswickians to take back. (Barnes p.178)

Had any such traditions existed in Kirkby Stephen, surely one of the popular histories would have picked them up?[17]

In the larger concentrations of population that did catch the plague, often running into hundreds of victims, the corpses soon proved an embarrassment for the usual methods of disposal and new sites were needed, some on the fells, but others in new areas of the suburbs. These tend to leave evidence of their presence in place names such as *Plague Lonnin* in Penrith, and those used for the exchange of food at *Meal Cross* and *Cross Green* there. At Edenhall, which for a small community was struck with particular force, a Plague Cross survives in St Cuthbert's churchyard, a pillar on a plinth, its cross encircled in imitation of the Anglo-Saxon manner.[18] Once again, nothing similar survives in Kirkby Stephen. It is all the more remarkable then that a recent discovery should cast at least some doubt on this singularity.

According to a tradition to which there is widespread testimony, more often than using a stream as at Keswick, communities afflicted with the plague exchanged money for the goods they needed from the outside world by means of a 'plague stone', i.e. an object carved or pressed into service that held vinegar, or some other liquid perceived as a disinfectant, in which money could be cleansed. There are two of these presently in Penrith: one on Bridge Lane (adjacent to an old people's home near to the Hospital, **Fig. 2**), and a second, perhaps formerly in a field adjacent to Grub Street (now Milton Street), now in the front garden of a house near to the Evergreen Community Centre and Bluebell Lane car park (**Fig. 3**). Plague stones survive elsewhere at such places as Eyam, York, Settle, Derby, Ludchurch, St Ives, Ackworth, Bury St Edmunds, Rylstone, and Caton with Littledale in the Lower Lune Valley.[19] And now one has recently been discovered on the outskirts of Kirby Stephen outside a farmhouse called Wintonfields, about a mile outside the town on the low road to Appleby. The house appears on local maps at least as far back as T. Jeffrys, *Map of Westmorland* 1770, (where it is abbreviated to *'Fields'*) and parts of the building may well be older.

Fig. 2 The plague stone in Bridge Lane, Penrith.

Fig. 3 The plague stone near Bluebell Lane car park,
Penrith, often planted with flowers, as here.

Broadly speaking there appear to be four kinds of surviving plague stones. The first and loosest group might be called the 'adapted'. These are often no more than boulders, perhaps already used to mark boundaries, some already containing depressions or faults in the rock that could be worked into rough receptacles. These seem particularly common at Eyam, and were used in the 1665 outbreak when the plague was brought from London, the inhabitants heroically resolving to immure themselves and thus save the surrounding country. The crudeness of the stones they used may perhaps be less an indication of any lack of skill so much as the urgency with which they were needed. Similar adapted stones appear to be located at Ludchurch in Astbury, Cheshire, as well as the Zennor Stone near St Ives in Cornwall and that at Burton Stone Lane in York.

In a second category existing pieces of masonry were adapted, as apparently appears to have been the case at Alne in North Yorkshire, possibly at Settle, and in Friargate at Derby.

Then there are the stones that have been manufactured especially for the purpose. Some have square apertures such as that on Bridge Lane in Penrith, which is a large block of some kind of hard stone, thirty inches square, out of which a rectangular dish has been roughly carved only a few inches deep (see **Fig. 2**).

The most common form of plague stone, however, to which the newly-discovered stone at Kirkby Stephen conforms, appears to have been constructed from a roughly-dressed block of a softer stone such as sandstone into which the mason's auger was able to bore a cylindrical hole apparently with relative ease. These can be found at Hob Moor in York (where there were originally four plague stones, one at each entry to the city), Ackworth in West Yorkshire, Bury St Edmunds in Suffolk, Rylstone in North Yorkshire, 'on Longstone Lane' at Little Budworth in Cheshire, at Caton with Littledale in the Lower Lune Valley, plus the second stone at Penrith (i.e. **Fig. 3**).

Fig. 4 The plague stone at Wintonfields, Kirkby Stephen.

At Wintonfields, the 16-inch square block is made of two stones fitted together, of which only the upper is drilled, and the aperture is 8 inches in diameter and depth (**Fig. 1** and **Fig. 4**). It has a drain evenly cut the width of a finger, and some four inches long, which can be blocked with a bung. Hence it is evidently made to a fairly rigid specification, and, like all such objects manufactured by hand in the Early Modern period, no doubt at some considerable expense. Since the farm was gentrified in the 1980s, when two further properties were created from its out-buildings, it is likely that the stone was moved to its present location, and there seems to be no means of discovering its original site.

There is on the other hand, no reason to believe that it was moved very far. It is of considerable weight and lies more or less at the point where plague stones could be expected i.e. a mile from the town and close to its boundary. There is in fact a boundary stone not far away on Beckfoot Lane just before it reaches the ford across the River Eden.

I have been unable to find an academic treatment of plague stones, merely the afore-mentioned compilation on the Internet; there is no mention of them in Shrewsbury's comprehensive survey of plagues. Barnes (p.178) talks in terms of Keswick's relics as of 'a tradition' – i.e. not backed by any firm evidence; Mullett too (p.124) says of the plague stone in Penrith it 'is accepted in local tradition as a receptacle for vinegar or other cleaning agent'; Scott & Duncan talk of 'tossing coins into hollowed–out stones containing some crude, supposedly disinfectant fluid, possibly vinegar' and Furness (1894) the 'so-called plague stones'. In other words, I detect a scepticism here that would rather leave such phenomena to the enthusiastic amateur, groups of whom seem to sustain these objects up and down the land.

If the town lacks parish registers for this period and there is no evidence for plague in the popular traditions of Kirkby Stephen, is it possible to find indirect evidence to corroborate that of the plague stone? A visit from the plague was a momentous event; would it not have left its mark on the social life, economic fortunes and population of the communities it visited? Is it possible to find such criteria in surrounding communities that we know did have the plague?

The Punishment of God?
By far the most complete record of the 1597-98 plague is in the parish registers of Penrith compiled and sustained by the vicar, William Walleis. These registers are a remarkable achievement at a time of great stress and personal hardship, and present between them a detailed picture of a whole Elizabethan town under siege from the plague. They give some indication

of how differently we might view Kirkby Stephen had its parish registers survived.

In determining the numbers who died in the plague, until fairly recently scholars have cited information recorded on a brass plate of uncertain authenticity now affixed to the east wall of St Andrew's church tower in Penrith (Mullet pp.113f.) giving the totals as: Penrith 2260; Kendal 2500; Richmond 2200; & Carlisle 1196. In doing so, they have attempted to reconcile the smaller numbers in the parish registers by ascribing the numbers on the plate to the rural deaneries and thus including their penumbrae of surrounding villages, but to growing disquiet. Adding in the country deaths cannot account for the differences, for they were so relatively few since the plague concentrated on centres of population; and certainly the numbers on the brass plate were too large even to be borne by the towns. Phillips (p.140) estimates that plague deaths in Kendal were between 40% and half the population, somewhere in the region of 1,471 & 1,631 deaths, and substantially below the 2,500 recorded on the brass plate; whilst Scott & Burns (2001, p183) report the deaths at Richmond to be in the region of 1,050 – less than half of those on the brass plate.

Penrith numbers are discussed below. No revised figure is possible for Carlisle, the largest of the four with the smallest reported loss, but it is reasonable to expect some degree of exaggeration even here too.

Mullet ascribes the exaggerations on the brass plate to the eighteenth century desire to make the plague into a warning against sin. Walleis had so announced the first plague victim:

'HERE BEGONNE THE PLAGUE (GOD PUNISMET) IN PENRITH'

Below the numbers on the brass plate is written:
'*Posteri. Avertite vos et vivite – Ezek.* xviii., 32.'
('To posterity. Wherefore turn yourselves, and live ye.' Authorised Version).

In Mullett (p.122), it emerges that these words serve as both a summary and a reminder of the full text in *Ezekiel* viz: 'Repent and turn yourselves from all your transgressions: so iniquity shall not be your ruin. Cast away from you all your transgressions, whereby ye have transgressed; and make you a new heart and a new spirit: for why will you die, O house of

Israel? For I have no pleasure in the death of him that dieth, saith the Lord GOD: wherefore turn yourselves and live ye.'

Mullet presumes that the *Ezekiel* reference was added when the church was re-built in the early eighteenth century, and that it accounts for the inflated figures, in an age less concerned with exactitude than with moralizing on the event.

There may be some truth in all of this, but I would suggest rather that the motive for exaggeration was less sinister. The greater the number of deaths the more significant the tragedy, much as it remains today when news reports concentrate on the number of deaths sometimes almost to the exclusion of the wounded and mutilated who, with perhaps a lifetime of pain and misery to come, are even more entitled to our sympathy. Mullett points out that exaggeration of plague deaths is found in other milieu such as Catholic Florence; Barnes (p.174) finds that Jefferson's figures for Kirkoswald of 625 deaths are far in excess of the evidence of the parish register of 55 (and quite a sufficient number for such a small place – although there is no evidence that these were actually plague victims).

Mullett would have been on stronger ground had he invoked an exact contemporary of Walleis, and writing on the subject only a few miles away. Richard Leake, a young man of 30, vicar of Killington (a village outside Kendal) and of Calvinist leanings, preached and then published a set of four sermons in which he denies the importance of natural causes for the pestilence and blames instead 'the masse and multitude of our sins, in rebelling against the holy one of Israel'.[20] Later in the dedication he specifies the primary cause of plague 'as grosse Poperie, and blind superstition […] that abominable Idoll of indignation, the Masse […];' to which he goes on to add (p.156) more conventional sins such as 'filthy drunkenness, abhominable whoredomes, open profanation of the Sabbath, unlawfull pastimes'. In respect of God's vengeance, he quotes a rather fiercer passage from *Ezekiel* than that on the brass plate, one from chapter 14 verse 13 ending 'thou shalt not bee purged from the filthiness, till I have caused my wrath to fall vpon thee.' We can only hope that he was not aware of his fellow priest's bereavement; for William Walleis, tirelessly attending on his parishioners just up the road at Penrith, in the very heat of their misery and oppression, had just lost his wife Elizabeth and their son John to the plague.

Christianity has so far had a very easy ride in Local History studies, partly because of the preponderance of clergy at its inception. We get little sense, even in more recent treatments of this subject, of the psychological torments occasioned by Leake's sectarian rhetoric, nor the physical horrors whose sanctions underpinned it: of the killings, torture and mutilations of Catholics by Protestants and vice-versa in the fifteenth and sixteenth centuries.[21]

Edward Wilson in his essay on Leake's sermons for instance, apparently indifferent to their actual content, invites his readers to admire his subject's literary style (p.155) and view the sermons as 'works of literature' (p.164): 'A simile,' he remarks, 'that starts rather charmingly – God is like an indulgent schoolmaster – becomes a terrifying metaphor a few pages later,' where 'the printes or markes of his [God's] correcting rods' says Wilson 'may have a [...] precise reference to the scars left on groins and arm-pits by those who suffered from [the plague].'

In a sense, the poor Elizabethans of Cumbria were suffering two plagues simultaneously – three if you count the Scots, of whom Sir John Clapham once remarked they were 'a deadlier enemy' than the plague for, he said, 'the plague did not burn crops and houses'.[22]

In addition to the carbuncles, blains and the buboes, the swollen lymph glands in the neck, armpit and groin, fever and high temperature, continual vomiting, diarrhoea and prolonged bleeding from the nose which the physical plague brought, they also suffered both intellectually and morally from the evils of Calvinism which, as Leake demonstrates, was not only an inhibition to the development of the sort of scientific thought which would eventually bring an amelioration of pandemics, but also their rabid doctrines went out of their way to set man against man.

The Doctrine of Reprobation, for instance, taught that as well as good deeds being no more than the sign of a bad conscience, neighbour should look more carefully at neighbour, not by way of sympathy but to discover what secret sin had caused his misfortunes.[23] It made men distrust one another and turn inwards with their pain, as well as live in continual fear for their immortal souls. Hence, reports the priggish Leake in his preface *To the Christian Reader*, the plague had led to the 'diligent shunning each of others presence' (Wilson p.157). Leake goes on to argue against the Roman Catholic notion, embodied in Canon 18 of the Sixth Session of the Council of Trent, that an 'absolute obedience to the law of God, & a total puritie from sinne' can be found 'amongst the godly in this life' (p.162), insisting instead we are all sinners whatever we do and must expect punishment, of which the plague is part.

Once Elizabeth I, a Protestant, came to the throne those with extreme religious views began to return from their havens on the Continent in Holland and Switzerland, particularly Geneva, and many began to work the way up the ecclesiastical hierarchy, (though Leake himself is home-grown fanatic). Here he offers his vision of the final day of reckoning (p.167):

take heede that with his third whip he scourge vs not, till blood run down from top to toe: when there shall be nothing heard, but a fearfull noise and lamentation [...] *they shall call vpon him, but I am afraid hee will answere in thunder* [...].

To us this may seem no more than empty rant but to the Elizabethan, denied any other view of reality, these horrors could be very real indeed. When William Vetch, just across the Border, thundered in one of his sermons: 'There are two thousand of you here today, but I am sure fourscore of you will not be saved,' three of his parishioners left the kirk and immediately committed suicide.[24]

John Earle's 'character', *A Sceptic in Religion* is satirical, as the convention required: 'Each religion scares him from its contrary; none persuades him to itself,'[25] but there is no doubt that it is a serious testimony to the degree to which many contemporaries had their faith shaken by the quarrel between Protestant and Catholic. The stirrings of humanism and science are evident in the ascription of practical reasons for the plague coupled with some conventional nod to the Deity. Thus whilst the Council of the North writing to the Carlisle Council says 'The principal cause of the outbreak was said to *proceed from the Lord's wrathe powred downe for sinne* [...]' it further remarks *'that it is the more dispersed by the recourse of people from towns and places infected* [...] *and also by the carryeinge of goods from place to place, without observinge anye good order* [...].'

A preacher at York blames the plague on the continuing rain, and ends merely with a perfunctory reference to the Deity: 'God amend it in his mercy and stay the plague of waters' while Carlisle Council takes a

144

position diametrically opposed to Leake when they seek God's blessing on their 'careful endeavours [...] for the avoiding of further infection'.

Recording the Plague in Penrith
The conditions for recording individual deaths in the plague cannot have been easy and, whilst Walleis stuck to his post manfully throughout, the parish registers contain a number of errors which need to be taken into account when assessing the severity of the plague. Haswell[26] noted one duplication and I have noticed two more: several entries involve more than one individual, and a couple of non-plague entries have got mixed with the plague ones – a drowning and a baptism. Furthermore there appears to be serious confusion in the earlier part of the register where the Vicar is attempting to distinguish plague victims from other bereavements where, as is customary, no details are given of the cause of death (the drowning above is an exception). On 7 June 1598 he gives up trying to make this distinction and recognises the reality – that since 22 May the last fifty entries have all been plague victims, and he inserts a note indicating his frustration: (*The entries of the Plague are of no value now, for all the entries are so marked, including the Baptisms and Marriages.*)

Burials for the plague victims begin with Andrew Hogson, 'a strainger' on 22 September 1597. The first local plague death, Elizabeth Railton, is buried on 14 October, after which plague and non-plague victims are recorded alongside each other, (plague victims with the addition of the capital letter 'P', as the Government required), through October and November, the latter slowly edging ahead, until 26 November when a worrying phenomenon begins to emerge. Non-plague victims are being recorded from the same houses and within the same families as plague victims. Now, where there is a sufficient lapse of time, this is just possible. On 17 January a son, Matthew Vepon, is buried as a non-plague death, whilst his sister dies of the plague on 27 April and his mother on 1 May, but there are six (now seven[27]) other examples where the association is much closer:

John son of Thomas Hewer is buried on November26th and is not marked as a plague victim even though, between Nov 10th and Nov 23rd four other members of his family are buried marked as with the plague.

On Dec 3rd, Elizabeth Watson is buried as non-plague, when her sister Marie and her brother Gilbert were previously buried with the plague on Nov 24th.

On Apr 15th John Dobson is buried as non-plague but Alexander Dobson on the very same day is marked as a plague victim.

On Apr 26th Richard Nelson of Netherside and James, son of Anthony Nelson of Netherside are both put in the fell as plague victims (and recorded so twice), but James's mother dies on May 1st said to be of natural causes.

On Feb 10th John, son of John Atkinson, dies of the plague but his father on March 10th, and his sister Jane on March 19th are listed as dying of natural causes, whilst an Elizabeth Atkinson on March 24th also dies of the plague.

Had Walleis had the benefit of foresight he could have cited *CCR5-Δ32*, the genetic mutation in the *CCR5* receptors, to explain those who did not die of the plague, but since this was not available to him, what criteria did he use and was he being well-advised? Why was he so concerned to keep numbers down in those early days? And could there be more plague victims being thus passed off in the register – for there are a further sixty deaths mingled among the plague victims from 22 September 1597 until 22 May 1598.

Two groups sought to inflate plague numbers. Firstly, the religious extremists who, having no natural power-base, sought to extend their authority by finding sin and evil everywhere, especially amongst their co-religionists, and secondly those modern commentators who regarded events the more news-worthy the more people died. However the Reverend Walleis, from September 1597 until 7 June 1598 and the death of his loved ones, was in the business of trying to keep their numbers down.

It is difficult to measure social reactions with any accuracy at this distance, and in a society without a police force or a standing army, but it seems likely that every new sign of contagion encouraged panic amongst the previously quiescent population, and threatened not only the subsistence income of a community but, beyond it, civil peace. It was not merely that markets, the only places in which it was legitimate to trade, were being moved out of towns, and thus leading to a loss of income to the authorities and many other vested interests,[28] but that traders were taking it into their own hands to do so, with the threat that it might become permanent.

In Kendal steps were taken to try to minimise the effect of the plague on trade. The Corporation went to the length of setting up its own system of recording deaths;[29] the document it produced, its 'true note', distinguishes those who died of the 'Infectious sickness' in a separate column from those who had died of 'other syknesses', and the corporation employed its own men and women to look at corpses and decide whether they had died of the plague or not, independently of the parish clerk. The corporation document, says Phillips (p.37):

meshes with known steps by the corporation to re-establish routine commercial life in the aftermath of the Autumn epidemic, and in the face of some panicky rumours about the epidemic's revival overtook the corporation's decision to re-open the town's market and close down the unofficial temporary market which had sprung up on Hay Fell.

The document is dated a week after the corporation's latest proclamation of 3 March 1598/99 to reopen the town's market, and is very evidently an attempt to influence the townspeople by playing down the plague, (the term used by the parish clerk), and instead re-branding it as an 'infectious sickness'.

Clearly there were uncertainties about identifying the plague, especially given the general ignorance about causes of death reflected in the failure otherwise to assign a cause in the registers. At Greystoke in 1578 'The same day was buried Margaret Sle of Hutton John wch child was suspected to dye of the plague' which in this case was probably typhus (Barnes p.174); whilst the Warcop register repeatedly uses the phrase 'which died of the plague as was thought' for the Blatarne deaths.[30]

Both Carlisle and Kendal employed professional visitors or inspectors to verify nature of the deaths. In Carlisle the city's medical officer, Edward Alburgh, 'who worked in co-operation with Edward Aglionby' were the visitors (Hughes p.56). A similar system seems to have been used in Kendal (Phillips p.137-8) with Robert Fisher and Ned Harrison initially the inspectors (Harrison did not survive the task). It is not clear that Penrith had anything similar to aid the Reverend Walleis, who also seems unusual in performing a task normally assigned to the Parish Clerk. After the first hundred or so deaths, the parish authorities in Penrith began to use for graves first the land surrounding or associated with the individual properties of the victims (interestingly using the term 'yard' which has only survived in America for these gardens and orchards) and then in the spring of 1598, as the numbers climb steeply, they turned to the Fell, the uncultivated land on the slopes above Penrith (as they were to do elsewhere).

Here, however, the implications are not entirely clear. The primary motive was obviously to relieve the pressure on consecrated ground, once the private land had been used up. It is also the last resting place of most, though not all, of the victims designated as '*poor*', as well as more than half of the servants. The evidence suggests many of the others who went into the Fell were similarly indigent vagrants drawn into the town in search of food.

It is not clear, however, that the criteria for the use of the Fell are altogether consistent throughout the progress of the plague. At first its use is only occasional, but then from 15 May through until June 1598 there was evidently an emergency in which the provision of graves was not keeping up with the speed of the unfolding tragedy. Almost every corpse is laid in the Fell, sixty or so individuals, after which its use is frequent but not universal, until August when it tapers off for the final 300 or so deaths. This suggests a considerable space elsewhere had now been consecrated for burials, possibly Plague Lonnin (Lane) though at no point was the use of the Fell universal. Even at moments of greatest pressure there were always exceptions that could be made, and space found in the conventional graveyard (perhaps family plots?) as would be expected in a strictly hierarchical society.

Leaving class largely aside however, what is striking is the differing treatment of wives and children: wives had an over-70% chance of escaping the Fell, sons and daughters only a 60% chance. Daughters formed by far the biggest category of victims (women outweighing men by 1.37:1), perhaps because of their greater association with the confines of the home where the disease was chiefly spread. That popular Edwardian song 'Your baby has gone down the plughole' when the angels tell the mother, 'not lost but gone before' may do something to prepare us for the callousness of earlier societies that suffered high rates of infant mortality – in particular the altogether less *affective* Early Modern society, which swaddled its children and hung them on the back of doors, ignoring them until they were three, and of which Lawrence Stone observes (p.81):

a population of which about half was under twenty and only a handful over sixty; in which marriage was delayed longer than in any other known society; in which so many infants died that they could only be regarded as expendable; and in which the family itself was a loose association of transients, constantly broken up by death of parents or children or the early departure of children from home. [...] Death was a part of life, and realistically treated as such.[31]

It was a cold and calculating society. Marriages were made to obtain wealth and power rather than for love, and 'The stage is more beholden to love than the life of man,' observed Sir Francis Bacon rather morosely.[32]

How bad were conditions in the Fell? 'The greater number of those who perished,' according to Barnes (p.173), 'were buried in a common trench or grave on the fell,' and one is left with the insalubrious associations of the open pits sometimes used by farmers at lambing time. Certainly there were plague pits elsewhere, but since Barnes is wrong in the first of his statements - for twice as many corpses went into graves in the town as were disposed of on the Fell - then might he not also be mistaken in the second?

Excavating the recent Elizabeth Line across London, more than 3,000 victims of the 1665 Plague were discovered near Liverpool Street Station. Daniel Defoe seems to have been responsible for establishing the view that the victims at this time had been disposed of without compassion:

The cart had in it 16 or 17 bodies, some were wrapt up in linen sheets, some in rags, some little other than naked, or so loose that what covering they had fell from them [...] and they fell quite naked among the rest.

Satirist and journalist, Defoe had an interest in the sensational in writing his *Journal of the Plague Year* (1722), but at the time of the Plague he had been but five years old and his material is taken from the memories of others. In reality, 'Far from being dumped' wrote Ben MacIntyre in *The Times* (December 2017), the bodies discovered by Crossrail:

were all laid to rest in coffins, head to toe, east to west, obeying the rules of Christian burial. These were clearly respectful, traditional interments, conducted at the height of the Great Plague.[33]

We cannot be sure of the practices in Penrith sixty and more years earlier, but the Reverend Walleis stayed at his post throughout the entire crisis, recording it all meticulously and presumably officiating on the Fell too, and there is no reason to assume he would have been any less respectful of the dead, (though the Fell would remain a bleak ending-place). With his wife and son killed by the plague (30 May and 4 June) and with scarcely a pause since its arrival in August 1597, Walleis was now in the tenth month of the pandemic. Down the road at Killington in the comfort of his rural study, the priggish Leake is drafting his sermons, four in all, delivering them from the pulpit and then writing them up for publication, apparently indifferent to the suffering of his co-religionists, denying the possibility of natural causes and putting all the blame on the human sin, (and the papists). Artfully by a show of humiliation, he announces smugly in his preface, 'To the Christian Reader', that 'neither I, nor any of the people under my charge, were infected therewith.'

Perhaps it was that Walleis meanwhile has some kind of breakdown? For just over a week after his family loss, during 14 – 23 of June, there is a gap in his records, perhaps omitting as many as thirty deaths, judging by the surrounding numbers with the plague in full spate, and then when he returns to his duties there are hints of a more mordant streak in his tabulation.

July 14	*Isabell Musegrave, basterd. fell.*
Aug 11	*Margaret Cowp(er), a wenshe. fell.*[34]
Aug 11	*one Edward Crawe and a wenshe of Edenhall, both buried on Penrith fell.*
Aug 19	*a child of John Penreth, buried closelie.*

It could simply have been his subject matter, or was he looking on his congregation and life now with a more jaundiced eye, and perhaps with an opportunity to review his faith?

In the light of the above, I would estimate the final total of plague deaths in Penrith to have been:

listed by Walleis as plague victims 'P'	618
listed as non-plague victims but from plague houses	7+
omitted 14 – 23 June (10 days @ current 3.3 daily average)	33
	658

Evidence of the Consequences of Plague
Were there social and economic outcomes left elsewhere by the plague
that might be used to test whether it was present in Kirkby Stephen? As it
happens, evidentially, the boot is now on the other foot, for we have
Margaret Gowling's excellent study of economic life in seventeenth
century Kirkby Stephen from 1605, just after the plague had struck
elsewhere. Unfortunately evidence from what ought to be the key
comparison, Appleby, a settlement of a similar size with 128 deaths, is
overshadowed by the movements of Lady Anne and the Cliffords for
most of seventeenth century; whilst Bouch's brief 1951 study only starts
in 1660. Furthermore Gowling's evidence (2005) for Kirkby Stephen
through surviving wills and inventories can only reflect economic
development obliquely. Inevitably, by following the fortunes of the more
successful individuals, it is all too easy to ignore her initial caveat: that
this is a society still dogged by famine and at best with only a subsistence
economy.

As to the larger settlements, there is serious disagreement amongst
scholars as to the short and medium-term consequences of the plague,
dividing largely along generational lines. Older critics are more inclined
to stress the strains (especially financial) put on the civic authorities
during the plague and to assume from the general impression given that
the plague must have had cataclysmic consequences. In Carlisle for
example, Hughes (p.59) talks of the dislocation of town life, the expense
and loss of revenue. 'The social consequences of such an epidemic were
profound. Many families were completely wiped out, surnames vanished,
old trades and skills disappeared'. Barnes (pp.177-8) quotes William
James, Dean of Durham, who laments the consequences of the plague in
the North country, the 'decay of tillage and dispeopling of villages […].
By this decay, the Queen loses 500 horsemen […] and colleges and
cathedrals are impoverished, because tenants cannot pay their rents […].'

Phillips (p.141), on the other hand, acknowledges that Kendal's
'population level had made at least a modest recovery within a decade';
whilst Scott & Duncan's more systematic 1996 study corrects Bouch &
Jones' earlier assumption (p.81) that the plague attacked old and young
and missed breeders. Instead the facts, they say, suggest: 'The age-
specific mortality corresponded with the calculated age structure of the
population and infection appeared to be random.'

They go on to say: 'The population rapidly build up after the plague, largely by immigration and not by increased fertility, and steady-state conditions were re-established within 5 years and continued for 150 years.'

In our present-day society, those trade figures which do not show a percentage increase on the previous year are considered 'disappointing'. By contrast, in an agrarian society based upon a subsistence model, they expected that things would go on, barring natural disasters, pretty much as they were in perpetuity; which is probably why they presented their biblical dramas in modern dress. In a town like Penrith or Kirkby Stephen, the land that could be cultivated had long been divided up and the generally static population, to which, say Scott & Duncan, Penrith returned for another 150 years, was a consequence of the limited land-space for food production. The brutality of vagrancy laws inhibited the movement of the young, so they had to wait for the death of their parents or neighbours before they could take their place as breeders; late marriage was the norm.

Thus in its own way, the plague was of benefit to the young who survived, for there were now vacant 'places' within the structure to be filled. The town needed shoemakers, smiths and all the rest, and the figures showed that 65 new families were recruited to fill the gaps (mostly from the surrounding parishes) and there was an increase in marriages, then of the birth-rate, with always of course the concomitant danger of over-population and its consequences. The speed of recovery within the Cumbrian towns was such that within ten years, William Camden in *Britannia* (1607) could describe Kendal as a:

towne of very great trade and resort [...] *a place excellent for clothing; and for industry surpassing that it regard thereof a great name. For the inhabitants have great trafficke and vent of their woollen clothes throughout all parts of England,* (Bouch & Jones p.136)

- although thirty-six years later Richard Braithwaite in *The English Gentleman*, 1641 pp.125-6, describing the same town, talks of '*decrease and decay*'.

Conclusion

On the face of it, Kirkby Stephen's singularity in appearing to have escaped the plague of 1597-98 is quite remarkable, given its status as a centre of population only five miles from Brough, where there were seventeen fatalities; twelve miles from Appleby, with its own substantial infection, and ringed by the smaller contagions at Shap and Blatarne, both on access roads to Kirkby Stephen. However, if the circle is widened beyond the county boundary, plague is not evident at this time in comparable communities outside Cumbria such as Kirkby Lonsdale or Barnard Castle.

Kirkby Stephen already had a market charter and was about to receive a second, but there is no evidence yet that it formally catered for visitors. Gowling (p.3) describes it as 'a small village surrounded by even smaller hamlets, a village of farmers with no resident landed gentry until the late sixteenth century.' And goes on to say: 'There may have been brewers, tanners and hosiers, though they do not appear in the rentals; they were probably secondary occupations by the farming families,' and a little later, 'Judging by the present layout, this was a village of farm houses and cottages around the market place and along the main road.'(pp.6-7). Inns seem to develop later, during the eighteenth century so it may well have been that the only hospitality on offer would have been in the houses of village people and therefore visitors perhaps fewer in number, (though in both Penrith and Eyam such humble circumstances seem to have enabled and perhaps encouraged the spread of the disease.)

Our knowledge of the period remains very patchy and the lack of parish records in the town is a serious deficiency. Even where they exist, our evidence of plague deaths rests on whether they were separately distinguished from the common practice of leaving the cause of death blank. Howson paints a picture of incompetence and stress at a parish level, with parish records unpopular and slipshod in the sixteenth century and plague numbers probably higher than those recorded. Thomas Cromwell's injunction, he says, met with:

various degrees of resentment or indifference, and one does not find any general striving after accuracy until late in the seventeenth century [...] and it was almost a matter of course to leave a permanent gap in the register to mark the interval between the death or retirement of one recorder and the appointment of a successor (p.29).

1596-98. This was one of the greatest epidemics and affected nearly all of the north of England. The mortality generally was high and probably very much higher than many of the registers indicate. One gets the impression that in some parishes the task of recording was too much for the recorders. Certainly in some large and scattered parishes many corpses never reached the churchyard [...] (p36).

Nicholson & Burn 1777, seem to give the first account of plague in Appleby and beyond the single figure they give of 128 deaths and the associated reference to the moving of the market, there does not appear to be any corroborating evidence for plague there – no plague stone, no street names, no oral tradition – and so the situation is otherwise very like that of Kirkby Stephen before the plague stone was found, and J.F.D. Shrewsbury, formerly the authority on such matters, describes Appleby deaths as 'inferential'.

I have deliberately left the subject of the Brough plague deaths until last, partly because they benefit from as much contemporary context as can be brought to bear, and partly because they are two-edged so far as evidence of plague in Kirkby Stephen is concerned. On the one hand they show how close the contagion approached, but on the other how relatively easily it could be contained and prevented from affecting the other *circa* 150-200 households in the surrounding town.

How was it that two families, each of seven individuals, eight months apart, that of Abraam Wharton in Nov 1597 and John Hodgeson in July 1598, could be surgically removed from a community whilst barely affecting the rest? (There were three other victims, a boy in 1597 and two females the following year, but they also may have been associated with the families).

As a small town, Brough is more than usually scattered because of the terrain. It may have been that the victims were fairly isolated in their domiciles (as they appear to be at Blatarne)? Wharton is a family name of local gentry, which might give some measure of isolation, but there are plenty of Whartons at all social levels in the town's history. Barnes is rather censorious about Carlisle's response to the plague: 'The lesson the visitation taught was a severe one, and precautions were taken from preventing the city being infected by strangers in the future' (pp.179-180), but in fact Hughes' account shows a high level of organization in the city, for they had already suffered a number of visitations in the sixteenth

154

century, notably one ten years earlier. Despite modern scepticism about the peculiar nature of some of the antidotes attempted – Virginia Cedarwood and Juniper were both considered effective for fumigation, or plunging hot stones into a bowl of vinegar – extensive practical precautions were put in hand to prevent the disease from spreading. Infected houses were sealed off, with provisioning of their inhabitants, and orderly arrangements made for the removal and disposal of the dead; a weekly collection of taxes was taken for those affected; attempts were made to have the prisoners removed from the jail; pest houses and isolation hospitals were set up outside the city walls; and a considerable number of people were engaged for these tasks. Hughes (pp.57-8) even goes so far as to talk of the 'thoroughness of the Authorities in their attempt to contain the outbreak'. We do not know how far such precautions would have gone in order to contain a single isolated family, but Carlisle's extensive precautions give some indication of the current ethos.

In the end, it may simply have been a question of geography. Scott & Duncan emphasise how far this disease was beyond its comfort zone in what they repeatedly describe as the 'bleak' Eden Valley. It could not remain active in the winter and needed the summer months in order to flourish, though in each site of infection it appears to have been able to lie dormant and then return; as for instance at Edenhall where a family of four died of the plague in early March 1597, and it then disappeared until July 1598 when a further 42 people died, and even in the smaller infections as at Blatarne the same pattern was repeated.

The key to the understanding of the epidemiology of the plague lies in the lengthy incubation period [20-22 days] *and, because of this, apparently healthy infectives could move around the country on foot or horseback covering considerable distances before they were struck down.* (Scott & Duncan 2001, p.134.) This is in sharp contrast to the bubonic plague or anthrax.

One possible reason why Kirkby Stephen may have escaped the plague is the relative contrast between the speed and ease of its transmission *within* households, where infection of one could mean speedy infection of all – 63 complete households were wiped out in Penrith – and its relative slowness *between* households, since the infection was operating at the extreme limit of its effectiveness. Hence when it arrived from Newcastle in 1597, it did not just spread willy-nilly across Cumbria but followed a distinct pathway, down the Great North Road, taking in Durham, as far as Darlington, then to Richmond, over Stainmoor to Brough (avoiding Barnard Castle) and then to Appleby, Penrith, Carlisle and Dumfries, which (in reverse) was the Scottish drovers' route. How then did it get to Kendal? Scott & Duncan (1996) on their map (Fig 5 p.12) have the plague bifurcating west of Brough (perhaps wrongly assuming Blatarne is part of Warcop village), and then coming via Kirkby Stephen to Kendal. I suggest it is much more likely that it bifurcated at Penrith, in a market town where contact through goods or persons was easier. Then, as one strand made its way north to Carlisle and ultimately Dumfries, the other made its way south, through the Lune Valley or over the high road from Appleby to Kendal, taking in Shap, and missing out Kirkby Stephen altogether; thus leading to burials on the very same day, 3 October in both Carlisle and Kendal, twelve days after the first burial in Penrith. Scott & Duncan (1996 p.14) amend their suggestion and speculate that the infection may have gone straight from Richmond to Kendal.

APPENDIX

The current evidence of plague deaths in the smaller communities of Cumbria 1597-98

Appleby
Nicholson, J & Burn, R. 1777. *The History and Antiquities of the Counties of Cumberland and Westmorland,* Vol. 1 (London: Strahan & Cadell), p.321.

In the year 1598, the market was removed Gilshaughlin, on account of the plague; in which year, between Aug 1 and March 25 there died in Appleby, Scattergate, Colby and Colby Leathes, 128 persons.

Within this parish is a tenement, now belonging to Sir James Lowther baronet, called Gilshaughlin (from rubbish shovelled down), where the market was held in the year 1598, when plague raged at Appleby. (Ibid. p.460)

Blantarne
Abercrombie, John. 1914. *The Registers of Warcop,* transcript, (Kendal: Titus Wilson), pp.58-59.

1597

Michell Mosse a child of Adam Mosses	*Oct 17*
Was the said Adam Mosse & two of	
his children buryed which died upon	
the plague as it was thought [...]	*Oct 19*
Margret Mosse & Agnes Lancaster died of	
the plague & was buryed in a garth at	
Blatarne [...]	*Nov 4*

1598

Richard Lancaster and his wiefe Jenet	
Wilson died both so *daynelye upon the	
plague as it was thought & were buried	
in their own yeard at Blatarne	*May 25*
Dyed Thomas s. of Richard Lancaster	
of Blatarne & the barne wherein he	
died burned & the corpse afterwards	
interred [...]	*June 6*

[* this is the only use of this word I can find, and I have no idea what it means]

Brough

Brierley, H (ed). 1923. *Registers of Brough-under-Stainmore*, transcript, (Kendal: Titus Wilson).

1597

Isbell d. of Abraam Wharton of the plague	*Nov 10^h*
Franncis s. of George Nattrasse of the plague	*Nov 22*
Mychaell s. of Abraam Wharton	*Nov 28*
Thomas s. of Abraham Wharton	*Nov 30*
these last ij died of the plague	
Abraam Wharton & his dowghter [...] of the plague	*Dec 1*
his mother & a *made	

* = serving maid

1598

Annas Hodgeson wid: of the plague		*Julie 6*
Grace w. of Thomas Waller	*}*	*Julie 7*
Ann d. of John Jackson sen:	*}*	*Julie 17*
Jenet d. of John Hodgeson	*} of the plague*	*Julie 17*
Elizabeth w. of John Hodgeson	*}*	*Julie 25*
John s. of John Hodgeson	*}*	*Julie 29*
Henry Hodgeson	*}*	*Julie 30*
Janet Hodgeson wid: ..		*Aug 3*
Jaine d. to John Hodgeson		*Aug 8*

[The last two are not specified as plague victims, but Janet immediately follows Henry in the register, and both she and Jaine are family members.]

Edenhall

Nicholson, J & Burn, R. 1777. *The History and Antiquities of the Counties of Cumberland and Westmorland,* Vol. 2 (London: Strahan & Cadell), p.414.

The parish register of Edenhall takes note of 42 persons (about a fourth part of the parish) dying there of the plague in 1598, who were buried near their lodges on Penrith fell, Shaddow (?) Bough or Edenhall fell, Flatt's close and other places.

['lodges', I take to be temporary summer huts used to supervise grazing; and 'flat' is 'one of the larger portions into which the common field was divided; a square furlong' OED.]

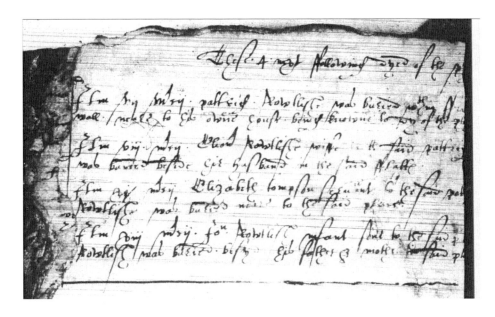

(above – from a microfilm copy of the original)

There is no official transcript. The following fragment of transcript is taken from Barnes (see Note 1) pp.176-77:

These 4 next following dyed of the plaige,

Item vii M'cii Pattrig Rowtlishe was buried wthn Flatts wall neare to his own house being knowne to dye of the plaige.

The death of his wife on the 8th of March; his servant Elizabeth Thompson on the 11th, and his infant son John immediately follow. The first is entered as having been buried *beside her husband near the said place,* and the last was buried *beside his father and mother in said place.* No further deaths are recorded from it until the end of the following July, with the following entry:

159

*July 29 the 42 next following dyed of the – * [word wanting].

He quotes another entry:

Itm First August one child of Andrew Atkinson of the plaigue & was buried in flats close. Itm xv & xvi August Andrew Atkinson wife iiii other children dyed of the plaige and were buried their Lodge on Edenhall Fell at a place called Shaddowbourgh.

Shap
Noble, Mary E. 1912. *The Registers of the Parish of Shap 1559-1880*, transcript, (Kendal:Titus Wilson), p.114.

1598
July the xvj daye. Robert Berket & ij children died of the Infection.

There is a note at the bottom of the page:

This year, 1598, was the plague verie hoote in Carlisle, Kendall, Penreth, Applebie, and all over the countre.

NOTES AND SOURCES

[1] Henry Barnes, 'Visitations of the Plague in Cumberland and Westmorland', *Transactions of the Cumberland & Westmorland Antiquarian & Archaeological Society*. First series, Vol 11, 1891; a seminal work. On pp.158-170 he reviews the plagues up to 1597.

[2] Michael A Mullett, *A New History of Penrith, Book II, Penrith Under the Tudors*, Bookcase, 2017.

[3] S Scott & C J Duncan, 'The plague in Penrith, Cumbria, 1597/8: its causes, biology & consequences', *Annals of Human Biology*, 1996 Jan-Feb; 23(1); 1-21.

[4] S Scott & C J Duncan, *Biology of Plagues: Evidence from Historical Populations*, Cambridge University Press, 2001; S Scott & C J Duncan, *Return of the Black Death*, Wiley, 2004.

[5] Ann Rosalind Jones & Peter Stalleybrass, *Renaissance Clothing and the Materials of Memory*, Cambridge University Press, 2000; Nina Mikhaila & Jane Malcolm-Davies, *The Tudor Tailor: Reconstructing Sixteenth Century Dress,* Batsford, 2006.

[6] The Gregorian calendar was introduced on the Continent in 1582 but had not yet been adopted in England which still used the Julian calendar in which each year ends at some time in March (the 24th in Penrith). This means that during the plague the first three months of each (Gregorian) year are counted as the last three months of the preceding Julian year (and vice-versa).

[7] Martin Holdgate, *The Story of Appleby in Westmorland*, Hayloft Publishing, 2006, pp.131-2.

[8] Rev R W Metcalfe, *The Ravenstonedale Parish Registers*, Kendal: Titus Wilson, 1893, p.126.

[9] Allan Mackintosh Maclean, *Registers of the Parish of Greystoke, 1559-1757*, Kendal: Titus Wilson, 1911.

[10] W G Howson, 'Plague, poverty and Population in Parts of North-West England, 1580-1720', *Transactions of the Historic Society of Lancashire and Cheshire*, 1961, p.40.

[11] *An Acte for the punishment of Vacabondes and for the Relief of the Poore & Impotent*, 1572.

[12] J Hughes, 'The Plague in Carlisle 1597-8', 1971, *Transactions of the Cumberland & Westmorland Antiquarian & Archaeological Society*. New series (2), Vol. 71, p.56.

[13] J F D Shrewsbury, *A History of Bubonic Plague in the British Isles*, Cambridge University Press, 1970, p.252.

[14] Margaret Gowling, *Kirkby Stephen in 1605, a Westmorland village in the seventeenth century*, 2005, unpublished manuscript, pp.18-19: 'In 1563, Kirkby and its surrounding villages had 300 households compared with Penrith's 140, Appleby's 227 and Carlisle's 450. Even in the seventeenth century various surveys continue to show Kirby Stephen as being larger than either Appleby or Brough. […] the Hearth Tax of 1674 , a tax on households and supposedly the most accurate of all, gave 468 households in the parish of Kirkby, making it around two and a half to three times the size of each of its rivals […] However, these figures can be broken down into constablewicks, so that the built-up areas can be compared. It then becomes apparent that the differences between Kirkby and Appleby built up areas is small, for there are 147 households in the town of Kirkby and 120 in Appleby Boroughgate. A contemporary observer, Sir Daniel Fleming, writing in 1671, comments that Appleby is 'so slenderly inhabited…and the inhabitants so idle' and Brough 'a town decayed and become a small village'. Kirby Stephen, however, he saw as 'a market town well known […] the market much improved of late by the trade of making stockings'. Back in the fourteenth century it had been the other way round, with Brough more prominent as a trading centre than either Appleby or Kirkby Stephen. See also Margaret Gowling, *The Story of Brough-under-Stainmore,* Hayloft, 2011, pp.48-52.

[15] C B Phillips, 'The plague in Kendal in 1598; some new evidence', *Transactions of the Cumberland & Westmorland Antiquarian & Archaeological Society*. New series (2), Vol. 94, 1994, p.135.

[16] J Nicholson & R Burn, *The History and Antiquities of the Counties of Cumberland and Westmorland,* London 1777, Vol.1. pp.321 & 460. See Appendix.

[17] The town is surprisingly rich in such histories, but none of the following contain any reference to plague: *Braithwaite's Illustrated Guide and Visitor Handbook*, 1884; *Parkinson's Guide & History of Kirkby Stephen*; R.R.Sowerby, *Kirkby Stephen & District*, 1948; Anne M A Anderson & Alec Swailes, 1985, *Kirkby Stephen*; Douglas Birkbeck, *A History of Kirkby Stephen*, 2000; Peter McWilliam, *Kirkby Stephen, Essays on the history of the town and landscape*, 2015.

[18] Charlie Emett, *Discovering the Eden Valley*, Sutton Publishing, 2005, p.91 (OS Grid Ref: 567323).

[19] On the Web see *Images of Plague Stones* and *Plague Stones* on Wikimedia Commons.

[20] Edward M Wilson, 'Richard Leake's Plague Sermons', *Transactions of the Cumberland & Westmorland Antiquarian & Archaeological Society*, New series (2), Vol. 75, 1975, p.155.

[21] Nor was needless violence and intolerance of other's beliefs restricted to the Early Modern period. See Catherine Nixey's recent *The Darkening Age: the Christian Destruction of the Classical World*, Macmillan 2017, which begins with the Christian destruction of the Temple of Athena, goddess of wisdom, in Palmyra, centuries before Isis arrived.

[22] C M L Bouch & G P Jones, with R W Brunskill, *A Short Economic & Social History of the Lake Counties 1500-1830*, Manchester University Press, 1961, p.16.

[23] Christina Larner, *Enemies of God: the witch-hunt in Scotland*, Blackwell, 1981, p.171.

[24] David Albert Mann, *Scotland...Almost Afraid to Know Itself*, Polyphemus Publications, 2017.

[25] John Earle, *Microcosmographie*, 1628.

[26] Francis Haswell transcription, with Charles S Jackson, *The Register of St. Andrews Parish Church*, Vol. I: 1556-1604, pp.126-34.

[27] Scott & Duncan 2001 p.135, report an eighth case, of the Smalman family.

[28] See Mullett p.13, on the activities of the 'metlaw and weighlaw' i.e. the supervisor of weights and measures, who made a handsome living out of it, an office good enough to be bought up by gentry; and Rev. C M L Bouch, 'Local Government in Appleby in the 17th and 18th centuries', *Transactions of the Cumberland & Westmorland Antiquarian & Archaeological Society*, New series (2), Vol. 51, 1951, pp.160-162, describing the multifarious ways in which market trading was supervised (mainly by fines).

[29] *Corporacion of Kirkbye Kendall A true note taken from the Clerk of Kendall church mencyoninge the nommber of those which dyed of the Infectious syknes, that and on the Kirkland, this Tennthe of March 1598.*

[30] Abercrombie, *The Registers of Warcop*, Kendal: Titus Wilson, 1914, p.58.

[31] Lawrence Stone, *The Family, Sex and Marriage in England 1500-1800*, Weidenfeld and Nicholson, 1977, p.81.

[32] Sir Francis Bacon, X. 'Of Love', *Essays*, 1625.

[33] Ben MacIntyre, 'Blitz spirit dates back to the Black Death', *The Times*, Dec. 2017.

[34] Some modern glossaries do not seem to get the measure of this term e.g. C T Onions, *Shakespeare Glossary*, Oxford University Press, 1958; & D & C Crystal, *Shakespeare's Words*, Penguin, 2002. 'Wench' could mean either a servant or a gamesome young woman. The joint association of the two, though not used here, was a common one, since girls were particularly vulnerable to unwanted advances when they went into service. Of the two well-known diaries of the period, Simon Forman reckoned to have had his way with every maid who entered the household, whilst Samuel Pepys did so whenever his wife was not looking – though he preferred his victims to be married, preferably to someone on the Naval pay-roll. See Stone pp.552-561 & Judith Cook, *Dr Simon Forman, a most notorious physician*, Chatto and Windus, 2001.

THE PLAGUE: some early remedies
Anne Taylor

How did people try to protect themselves against 'the pestilence'? With prayer, quarantine, and whatever simple remedies were available. The author has collected a few historical recipes – which come today with a health warning: do not try these at home.

Ring-a-ring o'roses,
A pocket full of posies,
A-tishoo! A-tishoo!
We all fall down.

This familiar nursery rhyme is popularly believed to refer to symptoms of the plague: the tell-tale circle of red spots, the carrying of a sweet-smelling posy to mask the smells, and the flu-like symptoms that occur before death. But Iona and Peter Opie, the great collectors of nursery rhymes, note that 'A-tishoo' does not occur in the early versions, and that the rhyme does not appear in Britain in any form before 1881, i.e. three centuries after the last major plague outbreak.

They show that originally the 'falling down' action was just as often a 'curtsey', for example in a version they quote of 1882: 'Here we go round by ring, by ring, As ladies do in Yorkshire; A curtsey here, a curtsey there, A curtsey to the ground, sir.' [1]

In Carlisle 'the plagg […] began in this Cittye at Mychaelmes in ye yeare of God 1597 & contynewed until Mychaelmes 1598' and, until the discovery of antibiotics, herbal remedies were all that doctors could offer. The College of Physicians recommended various methods of preventing the spread of plague, such as treating 'infected clothes' (see **Fig. 1**), and the 'perfuminge of Apparell' by burning Virginia Cedarwood or Juniper, and 'Correcting the Ayer in howses' [fumigation of houses], (see **Fig. 2**).

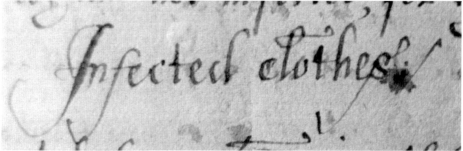

Fig. 1 From 16th century instructions in Carlisle on how to treat 'infected clothes', reproduced with permission of Cumbria Archive Centre, Carlisle.

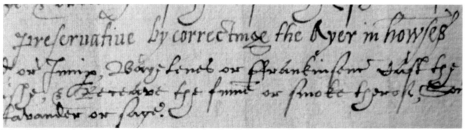

Fig. 2 From 16th century instructions in Carlisle to make a 'preservative by correctinge the Ayer in howses', reproduced with permission of Cumbria Archive Centre, Carlisle.

The instructions were to take 'dried rosemary or juniper, bay leaves or frankincense, cast them into a chafin dish [container heated over charcoal], receive the fumes or smoke thereof.' Other remedies 'to cure the sicknes' or to be taken 'in the first tyme of ye sycknes' included ingredients such as garlic, cloves, sage and wood sorrel.[2]

A later Carlisle manuscript is a *Receipt Book 1796*. This is a fragile, partly-bound collection of hand-written recipes which once belonged to the household of Samuel Goodenough, 1743-1827. He was Bishop of Carlisle from 1808 until his death; a very knowledgeable botanist and his wife the daughter of a physician. In amongst the usual recipes, for items such as Fish Sauce and Breakfast Cakes, are instructions for making cough mixtures, lavender water, medicines 'for an ague' and these useful instructions:

To destroy Bugs – FleasWormwood and Mustard seed – bruise & boil them in water a ¼ of an hour then add salt to your water & wash your floors & Bed steads.[3]

A well-known 17th century book of herbal remedies, still in print today, is *Culpeper's Herbal*. Nicholas Culpeper was an English physician and apothecary who published *The English Physitian* in 1652, subsequently known as *The Complete Herbal*. This work gave full descriptions of hundreds of plants, with a 'table of diseases cured by the foregoing herbs' and advice on making the necessary syrups, ointments and poultices. Contemporary physicians wrote in Latin, whereas Culpeper deliberately published in English so that those who were literate would be able to gather the plants and follow his instructions.[4]

For example, Culpeper described 'Crowfoot' (Buttercup)[5] and its application:

> [it] *hath many dark leaves cut into divers parts, in taste biting and sharp* [...] *it bears many flowers of a bright resplendent yellow colour* [...]. *This fiery and hot-spirited herb of Mars is no way fit to be given inwardly, but an ointment of the leaves or flowers will draw a blister* [...]. *I knew the herb once applied to a pestilential rising that was fallen down, and it saved the life even beyond hope: it were good to keep an ointment and plaister of it, if it were but for that.*[6]

Many plant remedies were used to alleviate pain and other symptoms of the plague, such as diarrhoea, nausea and vomiting. Plants such as Feverfew, 'the housewife's aspirin', which was grown commercially in London 1741 for medicine;[7] Willow, good against the *ague*, 'the boughs of which are very convenient to be placed in the chamber of one sick of a fever' and the natural source of salicin, the basis of our aspirin; and Poppies of course, made into syrups 'to procure rest and sleep.'[8]

An 18th century 'RECEIPT AGAINST THE PLAGUE', which appeared in a London manuscript *A Receipt Book of Cookery,* is as follows:

> *take of rue, sage, mint, rosemary, wormwood, & Lavinder, a handful of each, infuse them togather in a Gallon of white wine Vinegar in a Stone pot close coured* [covered] *upon warm wood ashes for four days or more, after which draw off the Liquor in to bottles & into every quart put* [,.,] *a quarter of an ounce of Camphire; with this wash your mouth, rub your Loins, & temples every day, Snuf a little up your nostril when you go in the air, & Cary about you some Spunge dipped in the same to smell to as ocation reqiuers.*[9]

Finally, the same herbs were also used to treat horses, as shown by another recipe from *A Receipt Book of Cookery*:[10]

A DRINK FOR A HORSES COLDE   R KIRTON
Take a Handfulle of Feather few [Feverfew] *a Little Handfulle of Rue,*
Two or 3 Spoonfulls of Anneseeds, Boyle these in 3 pints of Ale Then putt
in 2 or 3 Spoonfulls of horse Spice, the Quantity of an Egg of hoggs
Larde If dangerous putt the Quantity of a Walnutt of horse Allawaye
Sweten itt with a Little Treakle or hony & give itt the Horse Luke warm.

Acknowledgements

My thanks to staff at Cumbria Archive Centre (Carlisle) for several hours chasing up the two Carlisle documents quoted from here. Earlier publications either gave no reference numbers or an incorrect one, but the excitement of seeing the original manuscripts at last was worth it. I am grateful for their permission to reproduce the two small extracts here.

SOURCES

[1] Opie, I and P (eds), new edition 1997. *The Oxford Dictionary of Nursery Rhymes*, Oxford University Press, pp433-435.

[2] Details and images from a large, bound manuscript book 'Mounsey-Heysham MSS', Vol 1, pp65-83, CAC (C), D/MH/10/7 Box 59. See also Hughes, J, 1971. The Plague in Carlisle 1597/98. *CWAAS Transactions* Vol 71, pp52-63, and *Focus* 2002, the Newsletter of Friends of Cumbria Archives pp5-6.

[3] *The Cookery Book of Bishop Goodenough* 1796, CAC (C), DRC/61/2.

[4] Internet https://en.wikipedia.org/wiki/Nicholas_Culpeper

[5] Grigson, G, 1955. *The Englishman's Flora*. Facsimile published by Dent & Sons, 1987, p38.

[6] Culpeper's *Complete Herbal*, printed in London by Joseph Smith, no date, p8.

[7] Grigson, quoting Philip Miller's 1741 *Gardeners Dictionary.*

[8] Culpeper, p231.

[9] Rhodes, D, 1968. In *An Eighteenth Century Kitchen*. London: Cecil and Amelia Woolf, p52. Date range for the manuscript is 1698 to 1760, the book probably belonged to a Quaker family, the Bellers, in London. The original is now in the Hammond Museum, North Salem, New York.

[10] Ibid, p 17.

INDEX

(page numbers of illustrations in bold)